W9-BHS-849

PROBLEMS OF PEACE

THIRTEENTH SERIES

Particulars of the previous series appear at the end of this volume

WAR IS NOT INEVITABLE

PROBLEMS OF PEACE

THIRTEENTH SERIES

by

FRANK WALTERS
EDGAR ANSEL MOWRER
DOUGLAS REED
HORACE TAYLOR
IBBETSON JAMES
ALEXANDER WERTH
SENOR S. de MADARIAGA
ANDREW ROTHSTEIN
HENRI ROLIN
E. F. CARRITT
S. LAWFORD CHILDS
W. ARNOLD-FORSTER
K. ZILLIACUS

This book is based upon lectures given at the Geneva Institute of International Relations, August 1938, and is published for the Committee of the Institute

Essay Index Reprint Series

BOOKS FOR LIBRARIES PRESS
FREEPORT, NEW YORK

First Published 1938
Reprinted 1969

STANDARD BOOK NUMBER
8369-0042-1
LIBRARY OF CONGRESS CATALOG CARD NUMBER
68-57317

PRINTED IN THE UNITED STATES OF AMERICA

CONTENTS

Contents

INTRODUCTION

EVERY year since 1925 the Geneva Institute of International Relations has published a new volume of *Problems of Peace* based upon the lectures delivered at its summer school. Written by scholars and by statesmen, by League officials and by journalists of international reputation, by men of many nationalities and as many schools of thought, these papers examine most of the great international problems, political, social and economic; solved, mismanaged or neglected during the past thirteen years. They provide a working note-book, compiled in Geneva, of the attempt to substitute order and co-operation for anarchy and war.

But this year one problem transcends and determines all the rest, the problem of maintaining peace itself. Not a static peace, for that is impossible, "Peace" as Mr. Frank Walters says in his introductory chapter, must involve a continual struggle to meet and to regulate "the changing balances and stresses of international life." But to-day, as subsequent papers all too clearly show, in China as in Spain, in Africa and Central Europe, the world is in danger of acknowledging the supremacy of one law alone, "the law of the bursting air-bomb."

How that danger should be met the Institute does not pretend to say. It has never been and is not now the task of the Institute, as such, to formulate policy. The papers it now publishes present many different and, in part at least, conflicting points of view both on the immediate situation and on the underlying principles of international life. It takes no responsibility for any of them, but it believes that they will be of value to many readers who wish to preserve and to strengthen the foundations of peace and who realise the urgency of the task.

Because the task is so urgent the Institute has this year arranged for the papers to be published at a much earlier date. Already since these lectures were delivered in Geneva history has written a new and dramatic chapter in Central Europe. But for that very reason the papers on Central European problems and their relation to the wider problem of securing world peace deserve to be read with all the closer attention.

C.W.J.

NOTE

The date provisionally fixed for the next session of the Geneva Institute of International Relations is Sunday, August 13, to Friday, August 18, 1939. This session is open to all who are seriously interested in the study and discussion of international affairs. Further particulars may be obtained from:—

The Secretary, the Geneva Institute of International Relations, 15 Grosvenor Crescent, London, S.W.1.

The Director of the Geneva Institute Office, c/o The American Committee, 4 rue Adhemer-Fabri, Geneva.

The Secretary, the League of Nations Association, 6 East 39th Street, New York City.

CHAPTER I

THE PROBLEM OF PEACE TO-DAY

by

FRANK WALTERS

Under Secretary General of the League of Nations

FOR any serious student of international affairs it is very much worth while to visit Geneva and to see something of what is being done, and we who have the privilege of working here are grateful when people come here to study seriously the problems of international affairs. The Geneva Institute of International Relations provides a very complete and competent series of lectures but, by way of introduction to the papers reproduced in this volume, I am glad to be able to offer these few general remarks.

i. *A Tragic and Dangerous Situation.*

It must be obvious to all of you that the general international situation to-day is very grave indeed. It is much worse than it was at this time last year. Only ten days ago, when the House of Commons broke up for its summer recess, in the pronouncements of Government speakers and of the press, there sounded a note of optimism: it was declared that the situation was not so bad as had been expected, and on the whole better than six months before. I confess that I can see no real ground for such a view, unless it be taken on a very short range indeed.

I do not mean that we are necessarily facing an immediate risk of war, though words like those would be very much less exaggerated now than even a year ago. Practically every nation, great and small, is spending on armaments far more money than it can possibly afford, or than anybody thinks reasonable. So long as that situation exists, it is quite useless to talk about an improvement in the international situation. What is being done in the matter of armaments is the test of whether there is an improvement or not, and the present situation in that respect is the proof that there is no improvement.

The general subject of these papers is " Problems of Peace " and I should like to consider for one moment what is meant by " Peace." Do not think of peace as something which is, so to speak, a natural state of affairs which can be counted on to continue so long as nobody is wicked enough to interrupt it. Under present conditions the task of preserving peace means something very different. It means a continual effort to meet the changing balances and stresses of international life. Nations alter and develop, their population increases, their power increases or decreases, their temperament, desires and aims vary, and " Peace " means the success of the efforts which Governments have to make to meet those changed conditions, and to cope with them without disaster. Think, therefore, of " Peace " as continuous, active, I might almost say violent, effort, of which the burden rests in the first place upon the Governments, but also, in democratic countries at least, on all citizens.

This effort which the Governments have to make for the maintenance of peace may perhaps be considered under two particular aspects. They have to deal with the immediate day-to-day problems, and they have to try also to build up a basis for lasting peace in the future. If at any time the underlying basis is solid and secure, the surface problems can be disposed of without too great difficulty and danger. If, on the contrary, the underlying basis is shaky, the surface problems become correspondingly more dangerous and therefore, of course, more important. They may become so dangerous and so important as to distract attention altogether from the second part of the Governments' task, that is, the building or maintaining of a solid platform for peace. That, of course, is exactly what has been happening during the last two years, with ever-increasing rapidity; and at the present moment most Governments in their anxieties of every day have almost lost sight of the more permanent part of their task. So it comes that a momentary easing of the tension on the surface can be regarded as justifying an optimistic attitude for the future. But that, as I have said, is an illusion. There is no real improvement unless the underlying basis is strengthened, and the test of that is armaments.

Let us go a little further into this distinction between the immediate problems and a lasting basis for peace. What I mean by the first is evident enough: I mean such questions as Spain and the intervention which is taking place there; the war between China and Japan; the problem of Czechoslovakia; the problems of colonies, of economic necessities, and so on. By the second, by the durable basis for peace, I mean the existence of agreed principles and methods for regulating international differences, agreed universally or widely enough for practical purposes. To construct that basis was the essential aim at the time when the Covenant was drafted; and it was, in fact, achieved, not perfectly or completely, but well enough for most practical purposes. And so for the first ten or fifteen years after the war, the problems that arose from time to time were settled, permanently or temporarily, without too great difficulty, and at the same time the armaments burden was on the whole greatly reduced. Unhappily during the last few years the situation has changed. The basis provided by the Covenant has been shaken and weakened. Individual problems have grown correspondingly in danger and in difficulty, and now, although in theory the principles of the Covenant continue to be widely accepted as the right basis for dealing with international questions, in practice their application appears more and more difficult, until the gap between those principles, on the one hand, and the methods actually followed in dealing with current problems, on the other, is almost complete.

That tragic and dangerous situation is the background to these papers. It inevitably leads to two questions:

First, let us ask ourselves whether or not this situation is due to something false or wrong in the Covenant: in other words, whether the conclusion to be drawn from it is that the principles of the Covenant ought to be abandoned, and some other durable basis looked for in their place. Secondly, if the principles of the Covenant are right and sound, we must ask ourselves whether it is in fact possible to maintain them in the face of existing difficulties.

ii. *Are the Principles of the Covenant still sound?*

My own view, based, I may say, on a fairly intimate knowledge of the development of international relations since the war, is that the main principles of the Covenant have been proved over and over again to be absolutely sound and right. They have been violently attacked by countries who desire to be the sole judges of their own cause; they have been inadequately defended by others who feared to involve themselves too far in matters which they thought did not affect their direct interests. The consequences have shown very plainly how wrong that view was, and how directly, deeply, and vitally we are all interested in the maintenance of these long-term principles of peace. That applies just as much to countries which are not members of the League as to members of the League, and I think nothing could show more clearly how far that is recognised than these words which were spoken by the United States Secretary of State only two months ago. After speaking of the deplorable state of affairs in the world, the low level of international honour, and so on, he said this:

> "There is desperate need in our country"—these are strong words in the mouth of a Secretary of State—"and in every country, of a strong and united public opinion in support of a renewal and demonstration of faith in the possibility of a world order based on law and international co-operative effort."

I have spoken of the maintenance of the principles of the Covenant. Perhaps it would conduce to greater clearness if I say very shortly what I conceive those principles to be. I would sum them up thus:

(i.) Open consultation and discussion on all international disputes not directly settled.

It is fashionable nowadays to talk as though the Covenant system is opposed to the settlement of international differences by direct discussion between the countries concerned, but that, of course, is absolute nonsense. Obviously, the first and best way of settling international differences is by direct discussion, and the system of the Covenant is that only when they cannot agree directly do the interested countries come and settle their disputes by public discussion and third-party advice.

(ii.) The provision of methods for settling such disputes by third-party judgment, including provision for the reconsideration of Treaties which have become inapplicable.

(iii.) Obligation not to resort to war to settle disputes, and to join in preventing its successful use by other states.

(iv.) Reduction of Armaments to the lowest possible limit.

(v.) The constitution of an organised centre for international action, with regular meetings, regular procedure, and so on, worked out in advance.

To my mind, these principles constitute the necessary minimum for any durable organisation of peace. The present misfortunes of the world are due, not to having tried to carry them out, but to not having tried hard enough.

iii. *Can the League be Maintained?*

If you agree with me so far, we come to the next question, namely whether it is possible still to maintain the League in spite of the difficulties, and the losses that it has suffered in the last two or three years. Well, that is a question to which I am not prepared to give anything like so confident an answer. Nevertheless, it is, I think, still a possibility, though it is certainly very much more difficult than it was even a year ago. During the last year very much ground has been lost. Still, there remains in all countries—even in those of states whose official policy it is to attack the League—a tremendous mass of opinion in favour of it: often mainly inarticulate opinion, but you would be surprised at the evidence one has of the strength, the widespread and universal character, of that support.

I think therefore that there is still a possibility of maintaining the League, but I think it requires above all two main conditions. The first is that those who cared most for the League in the past, and therefore are most disappointed at its failure, should not turn away from it, but should devote themselves still with as much or more energy than before to bringing their respective Governments to carry out the principles of the Covenant. The second is that the Governments, and above all, the Governments of which most members of the Institute are, I think, subjects—the British Commonwealth and the United States—should adopt a firm and resolute policy, not merely kind words towards the founding of a world-wide order of peace, but a conscious, deliberate policy for its maintenance.

Though it is perhaps rash of me, I would venture to say that although citizens of the United States are much freer than we are in Europe from the dangers of what I would call the day-to-day problems, nevertheless it is in the long run just as essential for their future national happiness and prosperity as it is for ours that the maintenance of peace should be established on a secure basis for the future. In other words, what I have called a long-range policy is just as important for them as it is for us.

iv. *The Covenant System or None.*

The choice that lies before us and before our Governments is not the choice between maintaining the League and maintaining or substituting for it some other effective system for the maintenance of peace. It is quite definitely the choice between maintaining the League and returning to the complete lack of system which existed before the League was founded.

It is certain, of course, that the Covenant is capable of amendment, and still more, that the methods followed at Geneva in the past to give effect to its principles could have been improved upon. Nevertheless, as I have said, no effective working system for the maintenance of peace can differ greatly in its principles from those which are already enshrined in the Covenant. There is, however, a yet more cogent, practical reason for what I say. The Covenant exists. Even though certain great states have, for their own reasons, broken away from it, it is still the official code accepted by the vast majority of nations. Every country in the world, with one exception, either adheres to it to-day, or has done so until recently; and that exception is the United States of America, which took so great a part in drafting it, and whose people is at heart so devoted to the ideals for which it stands. But this consensus of agreement, overwhelming in extent, even though not completely synchronised, was due above all to the pressure of the Great War. Nothing less than the strain of that tremendous tragedy could have brought to birth, complete and almost full-grown, an institution so revolutionary as the Covenant; and it is perfectly certain that no new international system could be created under present conditions or any conditions which are likely to prevail in the near future. I am perfectly certain that if the League were now to cease to exist, my generation would be unable to build it again, unless—which God forbid—it were as the result of another world war.

CHAPTER II

AN INTERPRETATION OF THE FAR-EASTERN CONFLICT

by

EDGAR ANSEL MOWRER

Director of the Paris Bureau, Chicago Daily News, author of "Germany Puts the Clock Back."

i. *Historical.*

CHINA and Japan have fought intermittently for close on thirteen hundred years. It was in the year 661 A.D. that the first Japanese attack on China occurred. The Emperor Saimei sent his General Kotzuke with 27,000 men to attack Korea, which was then a Chinese protectorate. The invaders were met by the Chinese Emperor Kao Chung of the Tang Dynasty who, in a combined land and naval battle at Chemulpo, completely routed them.

For more than six hundred years there was peace between the two countries. In the next war, China, under Kublai Khan, was the aggressor. But Kublai's invincible armada that was to conquer Japan, much like that of Philip of Spain, was destroyed by a typhoon. Thus encouraged, Japan repeatedly attempted to pillage or attack China. This process continued up to the complete Japanese victory of 1895, when the corrupt Manchu-ruled Chinese Empire virtually collapsed and was compelled to cede outright to Japan all of Korea and the Island of Formosa as well.

Chiefly notable in this long duel was the almost invincible Chinese preference for being left alone (broken only when China was ruled by the anything but peaceful Mongol Emperors), and the incurable Japanese penchant for war. Each Chinese success brought about a prolonged period of tranquillity, each Japanese victory paved the way for a new aggression. In other words, the most pacific great country known to history, a fountain of art and science, was almost continually upon the defensive against one of the most bellicose, rooster-like peoples on the globe, and able to defend itself chiefly by its bulk, its riches, and its brain power.

The Japanese invasion of China in 1937 was, therefore, anything but a novelty. To the Japanese ruling class, a group of people who saw nothing amiss in the sale of Japanese children as factory workers and prostitutes by their parents, there was also nothing morally wrong in an endeavour to enslave and to stupefy and thus immobilize over four hundred million human beings by forcing the use of narcotics upon them. After all, had not Great Britain exploited whole generations of English children in factories: had not Great Britain compelled China to open its doors to Indian opium less than a century before? Morality aside, however, the date chosen for the new aggression offered evidence of a certain time-lag in the calculation of the Japanese military leaders, whose wits were never of the sharpest. For this last aggression marked an attempt to transform China's semi-colonial position into that of an undeclared but completely vassalized dependency of Japan, and this at a moment when not only China, but other Asiatic countries like Mesopotamia, Persia, Siam, and even India, had begun to emerge from their previous subordination to the conquering

Occident. The tide of history was running strongly against imperialism.

At a time when China was positively thrilling in the throes of a national re-birth, the Japanese continued to consider it something less than a nation, to mistake its intensely patriotic leaders for corrupt Condottieri and its heroic bamboo-hatted, umbrella-carrying, barefoot soldiers, for mere passive conscripts or avid hirelings. The visual error was clear to the disinterested, but the eyes of the Japanese were closed by the immensity of the national conceit. They were all the more determined that China should, before it was too late, be reduced to complete colonial servitude : it should, that is, develop little or no industry of its own, but instead, provide an inexhaustible source of raw materials and permanently servile customers to Imperial Nippon.

Now, it was not Japan's fault that China had, in the Nineteenth Century, fallen victim to Occidental colonial imperialism and it was to Japan's honour that its military temperament saved it from a similar fate. Nor was it the Westerners who debased the Chinese, or taught them the use of opium, or the financial corruption, the organic disunity and inefficient administration which marked them out to be the economic and often the military prey of expansive nations. Provocative weakness does invite maltreatment, and the Chinese were both provocative and incredibly weak. As George Sokolsky wrote in his controversial book, *The Tinder Box of Asia* (1932) :

"The history of the foreign relations of China is a succession of outrages committed against foreign lives and property, and all foreigners gaining thereby a wholly unrelated and disproportionate reward."

At any event, by the outbreak of the Great War in 1914, foreign countries had not only chipped off numerous bits of China, such as Hongkong, as colonies, but had obtained as trading centres any number of so-called "concessions," meaning virtually real possessions, in the midst of the most important Chinese towns. Foreign citizens possessed extraterritorial rights, controlled the customs and the postal services, impounded the principal revenues, collected permanent tribute, owned more than half of Chinese industry, had financial liens on all sorts of things offered as collateral on the loans the corrupt Chinese were forever asking for. Great Britain, France, Russia, Germany, even Portugal, dominated China, with Japanese influence growing from year to year.

As fellow Asiatics themselves narrowly escaping a fate like China's, the Japanese might properly have put themselves at the head of an anti-imperialist movement for Asiatic liberation. Instead, they chose rather to join the Occidental exploiters and eventually to go them one better.

In 1900, Japan was proud to participate with the Western countries on equal terms in "punishing" the Chinese for the Boxer outrages. In 1904, Japan fought and worsted Russia over the right to dominate Manchuria. When the entire European world went to war, Japan seized the German possessions. Then, in 1915, it forced upon China the incredible "Twenty-one Demands" the result of which would have been to turn China into an almost exclusive fishing ground for Japanese financiers, industrialists, and military men. Of the five groups into which the "Demands" were divided, China was bullied into accepting four. All seemed set for the permanent enslavement of the effete Chinese by Japan. Japanese troops occupied large sections of Shantung Province. When, after the Bolshevik Revolution in Russia, the Western democracies intervened against their one-time ally, the Japanese made a very serious though clumsy attempt to set up Jap-controlled " White " Russian states in Eastern Siberia and Manchuria. An unexpected obstacle to Japanese designs turned out to be the United States, whose Open Door policy had long been a thorn in the flesh of the other Imperialists. By virtually deciding the war in Europe and by bringing China into it, the United States did not prevent Japan from inheriting the German Pacific Islands it had occupied, but it did compel Nippon to disgorge what it had swallowed of Shantung Province. A couple of years later, American naval preponderance plus the threat of still greater preponderance enabled the Americans at Washington to secure British and Japanese acceptance of the Naval Limitations Treaty and the Nine Power Treaty that pledged its signatories unconditionally to respect Chinese territorial integrity and independence.

China was saved, but China was on the verge of anarchy. The Republic of 1911 and of Sun Yat-sen had broken up into a number of warring provinces, each dominated by a local " war lord." The nominal Central Government at Peking had no authority. A Russian-sponsored attempt at Communist revolution added to the confusion. Though this was the period (the early Twenties) when " liberal " Japanese governments claimed to be friendly to China, their friendship continued to take the form of financing, encouraging and using the " war lords " in order to further the spread of anarchy, just as they had used and then broken the first President of the Chinese Republic, Yuan Shi-kai, during the World War.

When, between 1925 and 1927, a nationalist Kuomintang Government rose to the top and instigated a vast outbreak against Westerners in China, Japan, that later champion of anti-communism, never moved a finger, for such outbreaks obviously promoted the disorder necessary to the furtherance of Japanese ambitions. Subsequently, when Chiang Kai-shek broke with his Soviet backers, the Japanese were enthusiastic. But when his armies began to move northward in an obviously successful attempt to unite China, the Japanese prevented them by force from entering Manchuria, already marked out for seizure.

In vain! The forces behind Chiang Kai-shek were those of national revival. Renascent China found assistance abroad. In 1931, Chiang's brother-in-law, the gifted T. V. Soong, worked out with the League of Nations a vast plan for the regeneration and modernization of the entire country. From the viewpoint of the Japanese, something had to be done or China might be permanently consolidated. The Japanese quickly picked a quarrel with the Chinese authorities in Manchuria and seized the country, setting up as a puppet Emperor the last descendant of the Manchus, Pu-yi. And when the indignant Chinese countered by a boycott of Japanese goods, the Japanese provoked an "incident" and, after much more severe fighting than was anticipated, eventually overcame the resistance of the Nineteenth Chinese Route Army at Shanghai.

In violating its pledges to the League of Nations, the Nine-power Treaty, and the Kellogg Pact, the Japanese were cynically defying the civilized world. Italy alone seemed possessed by a philosophy similar to theirs. And unquestionably, they went ahead with some trepidation, though their fears were groundless. The British Conservatives had long been aware of the obstacle that an effective League offered to imperialism, including their own. Furthermore, they were all hot and trembling with that "bolshevitis" from which they seemed destined never to recover. Under British leadership, the League limited its reaction to academic disapproval of Japan's action, and after the League sent a scholarly committee of investigation to China which discovered there just what it had known before going, Japan simply walked out of the League. The League, in its first crisis with what was then considered to be a major Power, failed. Its member governments were cynics, who mouthed a mealy altruism while secretly condoning the oppression by the strong of the weak. The peoples, insufficiently educated and all unaware that readiness to stop aggression anywhere by force was the kernel of the League and deliberately intended by the League's founders, shrank from anything so "romantic" or "quixotic" as an effort to save rotten old China. And thereby the door was opened upon a return to the naked law of the jungle and the great aim of a world ruled, if necessary, sternly, by law, went glimmering. The American-fathered so-called Stimson Doctrine of the non-recognition of territories acquired by force, though generally followed in regard to Manchuria, was later broken even by the United States when Nazi Germany simply jumped and annexed Austria.

Japans' seizure of Manchuria began an era of systematic aggression, much of which was connived at by the Government of Great Britain. In 1933, Japan seized the Province of Jehol contiguous to stolen Manchuria and declared it to be essential to the latter's defence, and set up semi-controlled governments in Hopei and Shahar Provinces. Adolf Hitler slaughtered German democracy and started upon a remarkable career of broken pledges, in one of which, naval rearmament, Great Britain became his open confederate.

In 1936, a Japanese expedition into Suiyuan Province in Inner Mongolia was only withdrawn when it met quite unexpected resistance. Italy, resolved upon violence since the advent of Benito Mussolini in 1922, finally attacked black Ethiopia in 1935, encouraged by Pierre Laval of France. League action, though tardily undertaken, was so half hearted and feeble that, though it served to dupe the British people into supporting the Conservatives at the General Election, it did not deter the Italians. Whereupon, the following summer, those two strong-arm dynamists, Mussolini and Hitler, joined their forces in assisting a group of rebel Spanish generals in an insurrection against a perfectly legal but faintly " pink " Spanish Republican Government. The pretext was, naturally, defence against " bolshevism." Sly financiers and ignorant old gentlemen and Fascists everywhere applauded mightily. Thanks to the pacifism of the French and the now almost open pro-fascist leanings of the British Conservative Cabinet, Germany and Italy were allowed to go ahead with a full fledged invasion of Spain whose ultimate victims could only be France and the British Empire. The spectacle was so edifying—Britain and France frantically preventing the League of Nations from taking any decisions against two bare-faced thieves—that the " third robber," Japan, decided that here was a game worth playing and proceeded to form with the two assailants of Spain, an " anti-communist " Pact that virtually made

Japan a part of the "Rome-Berlin Axis" which was claiming to dominate Europe.

The moment seemed well chosen for further rescuing the world from "bolshevism." Just at this time (Christmas, 1936), something extraordinary happened in China: Chiang Kai-shek, as the result of a temporary kidnapping and a number of important discussions with his Chinese patriot captors, made his peace with the Chinese communists and secured their allegiance. In ten years, from 1927, Chiang extended the rule of the Central Government he represented from five of the eighteen provinces, to all of them save those directly or indirectly under the Japanese boot. And even the Northern rulers, whom the Japanese considered their puppets, began to feel the wave of patriotism that was sweeping the country and to gravitate toward Chiang Kai-shek. For example, General Sung of the so-called Hopei-Shahar Government, became so busy in his native village sweeping the tombs of his dead ancestors, that he sometimes forgot to obey the orders from Tokyo. Thanks in part to Chiang's wise measures and his efforts at national moral regeneration, thanks to British assistance in stabilizing the Chinese currency in 1935, China in 1937 was actually able to borrow in foreign markets for the first time in its history without collateral and at a low rate of interest. In both the military and economic fields, the country was making enormous progress. Anti-Japanese feeling was growing along with self confidence. Having had to choose between unity or absorption, the Chinese had chosen unity.

What more outrageous "bolshevism" than this could be imagined! Tokyo considered the northern Five Provinces of China as already belonging to Japan. Was not

Japan pushing smuggled goods into them with impunity and thus defrauding the Nanking Government of fifty million dollars a year? Had not Japan set up an entire semi-official machine for the debasing of the Chinese and the enriching of the Japanese by the unhampered manufacture and enforced sale of narcotics to "Chinamen"? The Five Provinces were rich: they contained iron and coal. China, in Japanese eyes, was to become another Korea, a sort of second British India conceivably independent in name, but practically subject to Japan, with hired Chinese officials and corrupt "war lords" playing the rôle of the Indian maharajahs. Japanese industry demanded new milk pots to skim, Japanese military new and easy laurels. And so, following the tried and time-honoured technique of first provoking "incidents" and then punishing the Chinese for allowing them to occur, the Japanese struck at the Marco Polo Bridge near Peiping, July 7, 1937. Again, with the blessing of Britain and conceivably of Germany, Japanese troops invaded the coveted provinces while warning the Chinese not to defend them.

Now, of course, this was not the way the Japanese saw the situation. When, therefore, Chiang Kai-shek, against British advice, defied the invaders and sent his soldiers north of the Yellow River to defend Chinese territory, the Japanese determined to teach him a lesson. To them, Japan was fighting in "self defence"; in defence, that is, of its right to treat the Chinese as it treated the Koreans and the natives of Formosa. Japan had extended the "hand of friendship" to China. What did these Chinese mean by their "insincere" conduct in refusing "to be toads"? The lords of the Far East would show them. . . .

A new " incident "—perhaps deliberately provoked by the Navy against the wishes of the Army—conveniently occurred on Hungjao Road in Shanghai, and Japan launched a second attack against that international town. What had the world's most terrible soldiers to fear? The League would eventually meet and register China's protest, powers like the United States would frown, but none would go to war to save China. Had not Britain's Foreign Minister, Anthony Eden, told the House of Commons ten days after the original " incident " that he " sympathized with Japan's difficulties "? Soviet Russia had accepted a minor humiliation in June on the Amur River : the country was weakened by Stalin's too frequent " purges " and was caught off its guard by the suddenness of Japan's action. Besides, what had mighty Japan to fear from American pacifists, pro-fascist British Conservatives, timid French provincials or bearded bolsheviks? Let them look out. As so, blithely and full of beans, the Japanese militarists set about teaching China a lesson.

The historian may note with surprise how the Japanese leaders, remote physically and psychologically from the Western world, and neighbours of China, guessed to a " T " what the Occidentals would—or rather, would not —do, while utterly failing to foresee the all but unanimous reaction of the Chinese.

By September, 1937, two months after the outbreak of the undeclared war, the *Oriental Economist,* organ of the Japanese financial interests, could write that " Japan faces the most critical situation since the Empire's foundation." For the Chinese jellyfish had turned and its sting was biting deep into the pride and the body of Nippon.

ii. *The Phases of the War.*

One might divide the Sino-Japanese war according to its strategical phases. At most, Chiang Kai-shek, who immediately became generalissimo of the Chinese armies, was able to choose the type of defence that would serve him best. But the entire initiative was and remained with the Japanese. It must never be forgotten that they were determined not to go beyond a certain point in engaging their forces. Therefore, the war became largely a reflexion of Japanese political aims, though such secondary considerations as jealousy between commanders, lack of real national unity, and the rivalty between the army and the navy, were not without influence on its conduct. For this reason, I have tried to trace the development of these aims, even though they did not follow one another in true succession but overlapped and sometimes ran counter to each other. So far as an outsider may judge, they were as follows:

1. The first aim was simply to conquer and annex the Five Provinces, which were conceivably to be used as a base for a subsequent attack on Soviet Russia. This meant overcoming the local Chinese forces, driving Chiang Kai-shek's men out, setting up Jap-dominated puppet governments of corrupt or traitorous Chinese, as in Manchuria, and exploiting the conquest economically. Furthermore, it implied seizing the rail and road connection between North China and the Soviets across Mongolia. In a short time, the Japanese had accomplished nominal conquest.

They poured down south-westward into rich Shansi, the site of most of the mineral wealth they coveted, as far as the Yellow River, and almost cut the Lunghai, only east-west Chinese railway south of it and the only remaining connection between Central China and the Soviets in faraway Turkestan. But owing to the weight of Japanese military material, the invaders found it inexpedient to go far from the very few railways and good roads so that occupation took the form of a few clothes-lines stretched across a courtyard. Between the Japanese lines, the Chinese never ceased to come and go almost at will.

A Provisional Government was set up in Peiping, renamed Peking or Northern Capital; unfortunately for Japan, the quality of its members was so low that their influence upon the Chinese masses in the way of bringing about acceptance of the Japanese rule was negligible.

2. Within a month after the outbreak of hostilities, a second aim was superimposed upon the first. This consisted in what was called "bringing China to its knees." Therefore, a declaration that Japan would never consent to deal with Chiang's Government. And the landing of a large Japanese army at Shanghai to demonstrate in the face of all the world that the Japanese forces were irresistible. This proved to be correct in so far as the Japanese eventually took Shanghai by a simple flanking movement. But the Chinese resistance was so stubborn, the Chinese soldiers so unexpectedly courageous, the national reaction in China so widespread, that, morally, Shanghai remained a Chinese victory. Perhaps exasperated as the result of unexpected resistance, perhaps after serene calculation in an endeavour to demonstrate to the Chinese that they had nothing to hope for from the West, the Japanese naval aviators machine-gunned and wounded the British Ambassador, Sir Hughe Montgomery Knatchbull-Hugesson, at Shanghai, after the fall of

Shanghai. At Nanking, which was occupied in short order during a period of Chinese demoralization, they bombed and sank the American river gun-boat *Paney*. Both outrages were carried out with impunity and without serious consequences for Japan.

The fall of Nanking shook China badly; many of its best soldiers had perished at Shanghai. Chiang Kai-shek, upon the advice of his German military advisers, re-established himself at Hankow. Now was the time for pushing ahead and "bringing China to its knees." Instead, the Japanese high command dallied and lost precious weeks during which the Chinese recovered their self-confidence and made a strong diversion around Hsuchow where the Lunghai railway cut the Tsinpu line. So long as the Chinese were at Hsuchow, communications could not be established between the Japanese in the north and those at Shanghai. Nor need they have been, for each force was strong enough in itself, and had the Japanese marched straight on Hankow, they might have taken it in short order. Instead, while the Japanese navy established the semblance of a blockade along the entire Chinese coast of 2,150 miles, and occupied the Island of Amoy, and Japanese aviators started out to terrorize Canton by wholesale air murder, the army followed the Chinese to Hsuchow. This operation took time, during which the Chinese gained the morally important victory of Taierchwang, and it necessitated the withdrawal of nearly all the Japanese troops from occupied Shansi, as well as the sending of strong reinforcements from Japan. When Hsuchow finally fell, the Japanese captured a good deal of Chinese rolling stock, but the main Chinese army, under the Kwangsi general, Li Tsung-yin, escaped on foot eastward from the highly motorized Japanese, and then boldly recrossed the Japanese lines to rejoin the other Chinese forces retreating westward along and to the south of the Lunghai Railway. The thoroughly exasperated Japanese followed them up closely. The Chinese evacuated Kweitch, Lanfeng, and Kaifeng almost without fighting, but when the Japanese reached the strategic spot, stopped them by dynamiting the Yellow River dykes and releasing its furious waters over a vast area.

Meanwhile, Chinese guerilla warfare had been successfully organized over the entire country, and the Japanese losses in battle and behind the lines had risen to more than five hundred dead a day.

So far, the campaign had proved only one thing : though a heavily armed Japanese army could go anywhere in China it liked, the price in human life was terrific and China was as far as ever from surrender. The war aim again had to be changed.

3. The new one was to " ruin China." This suited the Japanese industrialists who were in a blue funk over the recent emergence of Chinese industries that could cut under Japanese industries as the latter were underselling the Western world, namely, thanks to cheaper labour. Therefore, the wholesale destruction of Chinese factories went along with the systematic bombing of Chinese schools and universities, the erection of commercial monopolies in the occupied zone, and an intensification of the narcotic campaign intended both to paralyze the Chinese and to obtain valuable revenues. Militarily, the Japanese gathered their forces for the capture of Hankow, the cutting off of British Hongkong, through which China continued to receive war material, and the driving of

Chiang and his followers into the remote south and west where they would be, to all intents and purposes, isolated. Then, perhaps, a fruitful economic exploitation of occupied China could begin.

Practically, the decision to " ruin China " was a meek acceptance of the Chinese preference for a " war of attrition." However undeveloped industrially, China's potential resources were admittedly superior to those of Japan. The trouble was that blockaded China could not export, and might conceivably run short of foreign exchange with which to continue its scant, but essential purchases of foreign-made war material.

After a year of fighting, Japan, in the eyes of most observers, was further from beating China than at the beginning, and unless the Japanese army could begin making headway somehow, or the Chinese funds became exhausted, the former was in danger of having to merge its previous aims in a new intention, namely, the saving of its reputation and supremacy within Japan. For, if the fighting were to continue indefinitely, social transformation in Japan itself might easily be the result.

iii. *Personal Impressions of the Struggle.*

Visiting China in May and June of this year, I obtained a better impression of the struggle than I had previously possessed. In a brief but hurried journey, most of which was made by airplane, I visited a great share of the territory on the Chinese side.

At Hongkong and Hankow, where I met nearly all of the Chinese leaders, it was clear how intensely the flame of patriotism was burning in this former home of corrupt and cynical pacifists. Japanese attempts at terrorization by air bombardment were proving as fruitless as they had in Spain. The maltreatment of Chinese women, the brutalizing of Chinese civilians, the butchery of Chinese prisoners, were steeling the Chinese people to greater efforts. The extent of the Chinese determination was demonstrated best by their cold-blooded flooding of the Yellow River plain, just as heroic Dutchmen once flooded their country in defence against General Franco's illustrious predecessor, the Duke of Alba. A nation was obviously being born, or re-born.

With the Chinese armies along the Yellow River in early June, I not only realized how great was the efficacy of the Chinese hit-and-run guerilla tactics, with its steady drain of Japanese lives and nerve force, but experienced for myself the amazing morale of the coolie soldier, with whom I lived for a few days during the retreat along the Lunghai Railway. Unable to stand up against the well-armed Japanese soldiers, walking where the Japanese were riding, he none the less looked upon the invaders with contempt. He had accepted and discounted in advance the loss of any amount of his country. But what did that matter since he would win it back when the Japs collapsed, as they were sure to do, he thought. Without proper commissariat, or ambulance services, walking barefoot sometimes fifty miles to get a leg wound dressed, or dying on the way with his bowels in his bamboo hat, he was none the less amazingly unperturbed. With small air and artillery support, equipped only with rifles and hand-grenades and occasional machine-guns, often carrying umbrellas instead of bayonets, with incompetent, sometimes over-conceited officers, these simple tireless fellows were in one way the finest of the seven armies it had been my luck to see. If through sheer weight of courage and numbers, like terriers around a leopard, they were able to wear down the Japanese in a war where there was no real front, but merely mobile units coming and going as in the European Middle Ages, what could they not do if properly trained, officered and equipped?

In the Chinese remote provinces, in Chungking, the new capital, in the cities of Chengtu and Kunming, it was evident how much China was united. For however "Chinese" the manner of procedure—and God knows they were doing things in the strangest way—the fidelity to Chiang Kai-shek and to the central task of freeing China once and for all from the Japs, was the dominant fact of national life. Certain Chinese leaders asked me to deny abroad that they had ever considered separate peace negotiations with the Japanese, but they did not need to do so. For I had begun to realize that any defection on the part of the leaders would probably entail their immediate assassination by indignant, patriotic followers.

The readiness of the Chinese to avenge, even with their lives, any treacherous connivance of individual Chinese with the Japs that by making the latter's task financially and administratively useless, was still further diminishing Japan's chances. Given ample funds and the right to continue purchasing war material abroad, China, it seemed, could carry on the war indefinitely.

But if the prestige of China among military men and throughout the Far East generally had risen, that of Japan had incredibly fallen. Foreign neutral military men of five nationalities, whom I met in China, had begun to doubt the quality of the Japanese army. It was, they said, a bubble that had been pricked, a legend that had been exploded. Though untried against any first-class enemy, the Japanese militarists had proclaimed themselves invincible and persuaded foreigners to take them at their own rating. And at the first real resistance from soft old China, all their inherent weakness and inefficiency had appeared. Foreign technicians found Japanese strategy chaotic, Japanese tactics obsolete. Against any real army, the foolhardy Japanese soldiers would, they said, simply be cut to pieces. Japanese airmen were no better than Chinese, if as good. The Japanese so-called occupation of China was a joke, since with a little care one could walk right through the so-called occupied territories and never see a Jap. This downward revision of the estimate of Japan's strength had spread to the rulers of nearby colonies. I heard of a French general who replied to the threat of possible invasion of Indochina by a Japanese diplomat, with the words: "Come on. You won't get very far." A year before, the French would have been impressed by the possibility. Throughout the Far East, certain facts were taken as axiomatic:

(*a*) Japan with those forces it felt safe in engaging, would have to improve a great deal to beat China alone;

(*b*) Japan would have its hands full in any war against Soviet Russia, still less Soviet Russia plus China, and therefore, would shrink from further provocation of the Soviets or of any other Great Power unless sure of a general war;

(*c*) In consequence of the foregoing, Great Britain and France could feel perfectly free to care for their interests in the Mediterranean and Central Europe without fear of Far Eastern complications favourable to the Rome-Berlin-Tokyo axis.

The real danger, men believed in Hanoi and Hongkong and Hankow, lay in the uncertain attitudes of the Western Powers. What were these attitudes? As seen from China, somewhat as follows:

Italy was Japan's only wholehearted friend, partly because she wished to build up a counter-balance to German preponderance within the anti-communist racket, partly because she saw the advantage to herself in the Mediterranean of a strong Japan in the Far East.

Germany had first tried to mediate, then definitely helped China, and was switching finally to Japan. German officers and publicists argued and called each other names for three hours one night in the bar of the Hotel Terminus at Hankow, over Adolf Hitler's sudden abandonment of China and his chances of ruining Germany. At the same time, Germany might turn out to be Japan's salvation, for by attacking Czechoslovakia and provoking a world war, it might prevent the Soviets from using their obviously growing force against weakening Japan.

Soviet Russia was the only big Power publicly assisting China with which it had signed a Treaty of Friendship. It not only provided the greater part of the Chinese war material (after Germany stopped), but was sending aviators as well. But it would not actively enter the war, still less attack Japan, unless itself attacked. For with each passing month and the weakening of the Japanese war machine and finances, Russia's position materially improved throughout the world.

France had been timid from the first and insisted on keeping out of the trouble: at one moment it actually stopped all supplies along the Indo-China Railway into China under threats from Japan. But, at the same time, it had sturdily stood up for its rights at Shanghai, unlike Britain and the United States. As Japan's weakness became more apparent, French courage was growing and its policy had become one of invisible, limited, but constant assistance to China.

Great Britain originally saw nothing amiss in the Japanese desire to take the Five Provinces, I have reason for believing, and its Ambassador (the same Sir Hughe Montgomery Knatchbull-Hugessen whom the Japanese later machine-gunned) personally endeavoured to dissuade Chiang Kai-shek from resisting. But as the monopoly intentions of the Japanese in the occupied regions became evident, along with Japanese military ineptitude, Britain changed to a double policy of seeking to obtain a stalemate that would enable its subjects to maintain all their political and commercial privileges in China. For this reason, Prime Minister Chamberlain, in July, 1938, refused to the Chinese a much-needed loan. At a certain point, the British, perhaps aided by the Germans, would probably try to bring the conflict to an end by a new mediation at China's expense, provided British interests were guaranteed. The lesson of Japan's weakness was not wasted, but London did not utilize it to strengthen its Mediterranean defence because Chamberlain preferred Italy and Spain to be strong and Fascist rather than weak and Socialist, even at cost of weakening the British Empire. Britishers in the Far East had little to say in favour of Chamberlain and were humiliated by their government's policy of not defending its interests.

The United States remained an unknown quantity. Roosevelt, it was felt, would like to intervene in favour of China. American public opinion favoured China obviously, but declined to give any real assistance. Meanwhile, American business interests were selling twice as much war merchandise to Japan as to China and generally profiting by China's sufferings. . . .

iv. *Conclusion.*

I returned from China with the following conclusions:

By winning, China would first of all, free Japan from those pre-historic-minded militarists who were making of that country, with all its artistic refinement and potential contributions to the world, a sort of international nightmare. Even more important, by discrediting militarism, China would so weaken the aggressive forces in Europe that they would not dare to move against the pacific peoples and world war might be avoided. Finally, by successfully defending itself against aggression, China might so reinforce the desire for collective action that, strengthened by the membership of the United States, a restored League of Nations into which all peaceful countries could enter, might again begin to function and this time, adequately.

A Japanese victory, on the other hand, would mean just the opposite of these things: namely, a Japanese commercial monopoly in Asia and new Japanese attacks on neighbouring states; the encouragement of the European aggressors, further militarism in all countries and, inevitably, a new world war; finally, the complete eclipse of the idea of any world order save the law of the bursting air-bomb.

v. *The Point of All This.*

And this brings me to my real point, to make which I accepted the task of preparing this long paper. The issue raised by Japan's cold-blooded invasion of China has not always been a moral one. Why should it be "worse" for the Japanese to invade China and try to enslave it than it was for the British to invade and enslave India, the American to take the United States away from the Indians, the French under Napoleon to spread destruction and warfare throughout Europe? Is it not true that for the so-called possessing nations to combat nascent imperialism without consenting to drop their own well established imperial privileges, is nauseous cant. Nonetheless, between Napoleon and Colonel Doihara something occurred, namely a four-year war of peculiar intensity and horror. On account of this war, the League of Nations was founded to combat imperialism and to make aggression immoral, just as cannibalism, kidnapping, and parricide became immoral after being respectable family practices. The League grew out of the conviction acquired before and especially after the World War, that the prevention of a new slaughter by establishing true international law is worth national and individual sacrifice and that it is more useful and noble to die preserving international order even in remote places like Kamchatka or Patagonia, than in upholding the right of Americans to cut mahogany trees in Nicaragua. In other words, that war had become obnoxious, intolerable, and incompatible with the further existence of what we call civilization. Japan, Germany and Italy signed the League Covenant and promised to forego assaulting their neighbours.

This first attempt to make aggression immoral failed: partly through the stupidity and selfishness of the so-called victors in the late War (or their real internal rulers); partly through their generosity and unwillingness to compel their chief opponent to bow down and serve; partly through the moral unripeness of certain warlike peoples; but mostly, I feel, through lack of imagination and courage in all of us everywhere who cared for the new idea. We failed to make it clear that the existence of a League of Nations must necessarily be a heroic existence for which the best of us might have to die; that peace might demand constraint and constraint its martyrs. Perhaps we had lost faith in our own ideals: in simple ancient things like mercy and justice and abstract truth, like individual freedom, democracy and a little human brotherhood. In any case, we failed, And, just as surely our present adversaries, the back-to-the-caves, openly selfish and aggressive peoples and Governments with their joy in persecution, bloodshed and tribal gods, are restoring this faith to many of us. Thereby they are compelling us to accept that more heroic attitude we failed to produce at the right time.

I think the restoration of this faith and courage is the most important task of the present moment. I think it is so important that it dwarfs everything else in our lives, personal as well as cultural. The experience of Ethiopia, Spain, and even more, China, shows, in my eyes, what we must expect if we fail to establish the new morality which makes armed aggression, whether of nation or individual, a crime. A crime to be not only abhorred but repressed, by violence if necessary. This attitude obviously implies the sharing of at least some of the fruits of ancient aggression. But it emphatically does not mean that British colonies, for instance, are to be transferred under threat of violence, to new and probably worse masters. It means that the benefits of colonies, if any, are to be shared while the colonial peoples are being trained to be independent. It does not mean encouraging new aggression by yielding to bluff or blackmail or intimidation. Just the contrary. Determination to resist has always been the only successful method of dealing with a bully. But determination to resist—despite our Aldous Huxleys and other peace-at-any-price people—is not the same as desire to fight or belief that fighting is holy or proper or entertaining. Determination to resist is to-day a necessity unless the rule of the world is to be abandoned to savages, immoralists, morons and maniacs. But to resist successfully, we must have something worth defending. That something, as I see it, can only be a new and better international morality, the desire for an improved world. It must be a human ascent and not a reversion to the Palaeolithic.

CHAPTER III

CENTRAL EUROPE
THE POLITICAL PROBLEM

by

DOUGLAS REED

Danubian Press Correspondent. Author of "Insanity Fair"

i. *Retrospect.*

THE title of my paper is "Central Europe—the political problem." A rather prosy name for a —to me—fascinating subject. Behind those five dull words I see great countries striving to extend their boundaries and small ones striving to preserve their freedom, and between them all the Danube smoothly but urgently going from the Black Forest to the Black Sea, past Roman ruins and Turkish citadels, past the wooded hills of the Wachau and the rich fields of the Hungarian Plain, past German and Austrian and Czechoslovak and Hungarian and Yugoslav and Rumanian and Bulgarian lands. When I read those five prosy words, "Central Europe—the political problem," I see Hitler, with the spotlight on him, leaning out of the window of the Reichskanzlei in Berlin on the night of January 30th, 1933, when he was made Chancellor; I see Schuschnigg, just a year ago, sitting beside me in Vienna while we of the foreign press raised our glasses to him and wished him "good health and good fortune in the coming year" —a year that was to bring him ignominy and imprisonment; I see Benesh at work in the castle of the Kings of

Bohemia on the hilltop in Prague, where I sat and talked to him not long ago, with the silver Moldau curving by below, under its ancient bridges; I see Admiral Horthy, trustee for the vacant Hungarian throne, going from the Palace to the Coronation Church behind the priests carrying the right hand of Saint Stephen, the first crowned King of Hungary, who received his crown from the Pope 900 years ago; I see the boy King Peter of Yugoslavia walking behind the coffin of his murdered father in Belgrade; King Carol of Rumania, in the white cloak of Saint Michael the Brave, reviewing his troops; King Boris of Bulgaria, looking out from the windows of his little palace in distant Sofia upon this turbulent Europe of ours in 1938.

Fade out this prosy sub-title, "Central Europe—the political problem," and a rich pageant of places and people and human hopes and fears appears on the screen before you.

What is the political problem of Central Europe? You can put it in a single word—Germany. Is this great nation going to expand? Who would care to-day to answer No to that question? Then in what direction is it going to expand? Do not the events of recent months and years give the answer? I remember that more than two years ago, after Germany had re-occupied her Rhineland, a London newspaper wrote, "The seizure of the Rhineland leaves Austria and Czechoslovakia feeling like patients in a dentist's waiting-room." Was not this a succinct forecast? Austria has gone; the struggle for Czechoslovakia is joined. The line of the Danube points the direction of the expansionist drive.

In the jumble of day-to-day news, the confusion of

reports of petty incidents which are news to-day but are trifles in the great march of history, the onlooker's sight and judgment are often fogged. Look back along the years since the war and everything that has happened in Germany resolves itself into one simple process—the struggle of a manacled giant to free himself, to build himself a new stronghold, and then to look abroad for new domains to rule. I remember travelling behind von Hindenburg when he made his triumphal tour of the Rhineland after the Allied troops had been withdrawn. At one village his car passed under an archway on top of which young men, fine young fellows wearing only shorts, were grouped around a central figure that held a sword aloft in a hand from which a broken fetter hung.

That was the symbol of the end of the first phase—liberation. The next phase was to build a stronghold secure against all comers. That phase was finished with the proclamation of conscription, the seizure of the Rhineland and the construction of fortifications in the west. With that the German giant was once more secure in his own household. Now came the third phase—the feeling of biceps, the peering forth for fresh fields to conquer, the foray. Austria was the first booty.

This brief retrospect will show you why the Rhine, which for 18 years after the war was seldom absent from the front pages of the world's newspapers, has now passed from them, and why the Danube, which in those years was little heard of, has now taken its place in the headlines. With the Rhineland recovered and refortified all is well in the west. With the annexation of Austria the south is secure. The battering ram that is German policy inevitably slews round and points down the Danube;

the spotlight, the moving finger of our contemporary times, shifts from Vienna to Prague—to Budapest—to . . . well, let us wait and see.

Is there any other outlet for the energy of eighty millions of the most efficient, hardest working, most intelligent and thriftiest people in Europe? Until a few years ago my private opinion was that as the price of her collaboration in a general arms limitation agreement and an all-round, mutual, watertight undertaking to combine against any peacebreaker, Germany should have her colonies restored to her. I do not know whether they would have been enough for her to work off her surplus energy in, but they might, and it was worth trying. But in these latter years too many treaties have been broken for anyone to have faith in a new one, and armaments are so colossal that the temptation to their possessors to take what they want by the use of them is almost irresistible. That chance has been lost.

ii. *Germany's Intentions in Danubia.*

Now the German bid to dominate Danubia is on. When I was in Vienna I sometimes travelled to Bratislava, in Czechoslovakia, by the tram which starts from the Ringstrasse, not far from the Opera. The idea of going from one country to another by tram tickled my fancy, for some reason, and one thing about that tram always interested me and set my imagination working. It announced itself as going, not to Bratislava, but to Pressburg, which is the German name of Bratislava, for in the days of the Austro-Hungarian Empire the town, pleasantly situated on the Danube about forty miles below

Vienna, had been much favoured by retired officials and the like as a place of residence not too far from the capital, a sort of Austrian Windsor. Now, years after the war, this Vienna tram still refused to recognise the peace treaty and persisted in going to " Pressburg," not to " Bratislava." This amused me at the time and I used to wonder how long it would be before the tram would resign itself to the fact that Pressburg had changed its name to Bratislava.

Well now, since that evening a few months back when I watched the German mechanized armies roaring down the Ringstrasse in Vienna, German troops stand at the frontier and could almost toss a stone into Bratislava. And who would swear to-day that Bratislava may not soon be Pressburg again? Or Pozsony, if the Hungarians, who regard it as a Hungarian city, have their way?

In what form is this German drive down the Danube going to continue? It is a tremendous force, this urge to power and expansion of eighty millions of Germans sitting in the middle of Europe; you might call it an irrestible force. In Czechoslovakia it has as yet met the immovable object. Something must give, sooner or later. In England there is, I believe, among students of politics a strong school which favours German expansion down the Danube, on the ground that Germany must expand somewhere and cannot be prevented from doing so, and that the process would best be diverted in a direction in which it would eventually bring her up against the colossus Russia and would use up much German strength and time. The theory of this school, attractive superficially, is that a nation of Germany's might and quality should not be prevented from attaining a place, in relation to the small States of Danubian Europe, comparable with that which the United States enjoys in relation to the Central American Republics or England in relation to the States of the British Commonwealth.

If Germany only aimed, in Danubian Europe, at being able to count on obtaining from these small countries the essential raw materials and foodstuffs that she needs, in peace as in war, and at ensuring that they should never be on the side of her enemies in war, it would be difficult to pick holes in this theory. But would the process stop there? Would it not irresistibly continue until the small States had been totally submerged? The whole history of the small Danubian States is of a ceaseless struggle against alien domination—Tartar, Turkish, German—and of centuries of alien rule. One of the few real achievements of the World War is—or was generally accepted to be until recent years—the liberation of these small States from foreign rule. The World War itself was born of their hatred of alien rule. The shot that was fired at Serajevo was probably meant to start a World War, in which the great Austro-Hungarian Empire should perish.

So it seems inevitable that if the German drive down the Danube were to lead to the renewed subjugation of small nations this in turn would sow the seeds of new wars. Does the German drive down the Danube mean this? Czechoslovakia is the test case. The Rhineland, the Saar, Austria, all these were Germanic lands, their seizure fits into the four corners of National Socialist doctrine. Germany won the World War on March 11th, because since that day her territory in Europe has been greater than before the World War, but none could say that she had up to that time sacrificed a free people to her thirst for power.

Central Europe—The Political Problem

iii. *Czechoslovakia—the Test Case.*

Now for the first time, the real test arises—Czechoslovakia. Here is a small but free nation. Germany, through her ruler Hitler, claims that she is only concerned for the welfare of the Germans living in Czechoslovakia and does not desire to destroy the Czechoslovak State. The Czechoslovaks are convinced that she does desire to destroy the Czechoslovak State; that she is determined not to have at her door either a little democracy or an ally of the country which Hitler in his book describes as the mortal foe of Germany, the enemy which must be destroyed—France. If the dispute is really only about the Sudetic Germans, say the Czechoslovaks, then why is nothing ever heard from Germany about the wrongs of the Germans in Poland or Italy or Hungary, who have far fewer rights than the Germans in Czechoslovakia? And, arguing thus, the Czechoslovaks come to the conclusion that the real aim is to force them to renounce their democratic system, their alliances with France and Russia, and to reduce them to vassaldom.

Time, and I should imagine a fairly short time, will show who is right. There is a great historic struggle going on in Prague, the story of which will one day make the most fascinating reading. The Czechoslovaks have now been diplomatically besieged for nearly six months, and the strain on their nerves must be terrific. Some signs of it are beginning to show; for instance, the resigned and almost despairing comments which followed the announcement of Lord Runciman's mission, and last week's manifesto of the League of Czech Officers, which very much recalls the famous salutation of the Roman gladiators—

" Hail, mighty Caesar. . . ." The Czech officers, " in the front rank of those consecrated to death," demanded that not a single further concession in word or deed should be made, since in their present position they could " work and fight and die," but retreat from it would mean the end of them.

To understand the despondency of the Czechoslovaks at Lord Runciman's mission you must realize that they do not believe the grievances of the Sudeten-Germans to be the real issue at all, but simply the pretext for attacking them, the lever by means of which their State is to be prized asunder. Believing that, they consequently believe that it is the aim of the Sudetic Germans,. not to reach a compromise with them, but by all means to avoid agreement and to push them from concession to concession until their State collapses beneath them. Believing that again, they ask what Lord Runciman can possibly do, and fear that he may urge them to make concessions which they feel fatal to their freedom.

I was in Czechoslovakia at the time they carried out their midnight mobilization, in May, in the belief that they might be attacked. It was extraordinary to see how this small country contrived in a few hours to man its defences, from the line of machine-gun nests near the frontier to the ring of aircraft squadrons, listening machines, searchlights and anti-aircraft batteries round Prague. Whether an attack really impended or not I do not know; but I do know that if the mobilization had not been carried out the authority of the Czechoslovak State would probably have collapsed and the ideal pretext for intervention would then have offered, for in the German districts Czechoslovak officers, who had been instructed at all costs to avoid friction, were being spat on in the streets. When the mobilization came the German population saw that intervention from outside would mean heavy fighting in the German-inhabited districts, and order was immediately restored.

I was astonished at that time by the quiet confidence of the Czechoslovaks, for the odds against them seemed overwhelming, their strategic position is desperate, their friends are lukewarm and far away. Yet they were tranquil and resolute. They saw a danger that they recognized and were ready to face it. They are not quite so comfortable now. They feel that they are getting tangled up, like Laocoon, in the toils of negotiation, on a false issue, and they fear that they are being ushered, in a gentlemanly way, towards the slippery slope of concession in matters vital to the state. " Better the devil that you know, than the devil that you don't know." That is no reflection on Lord Runciman, who when I saw him in Prague recently, certainly had nothing demoniac about him. But the Czechoslovaks felt happier in May.

All Danubia is intently watching this struggle for Czechoslovakia. Just as the battering-ram of German policy, once Austria was finished, swivelled round and bore down on Czechoslovakia, so would it swivel round again and bear down in another direction if Czechoslovakia were finished. Just as the annexation of Austria sent the hopes and spirits of the Germans in Czechoslovakia rocketing skyhigh, so would a German triumph in Czechoslovakia produce an immediate ferment among the German populations and among the indigenous National Socialist movements in Hungary and Rumania. In both these countries at present these movements are either kept under firm control or are forbidden. In Hungary the "Hungarist" leader Major Franz Szalasi lies in prison, and in Rumania the Iron Guard leader Corneliu Codreanux is in penal servitude.

iv. *Germany's Economic Domination of Danubia.*

What seems to me to be going on in Danubian Europe is an attempt, conscious or unconscious, to reimpose a Germanic domination, in some form or other, on the peoples of the fertile Danube valley. Before the war nearly all these peoples were the servants of one or other branch of the great Germanic family. Germany ruled over a large part of present-day Poland. Austria, the other branch, ruled over another part of Poland, all of what is now Czechoslovakia, a substantial part of what are now Yugoslavia and Rumania. It was a divided domination, and this may have been a chief cause of its collapse. You remember how bitterly Hitler in his book attacks the old Habsburg Empire and how fervently he argues that it must disappear and all the Germans be united under North German rule. He has nearly accomplished this. Does he intend to go further and re-establish, under this much stronger centralized and unified leadership in Berlin, the Germanic domination over the Danubian peoples?

Czechoslovakia again is the test. Bear in mind the great value and attraction of the Danubian lands to a great Germanic Empire bred night and day to the martial ideal. Germany to-day probably has the finest fighting machine the world has ever seen. Hitler used that phrase to me, when I saw him some years ago, to describe the pre-war German Army, and he left no doubt in my mind that the new German Army he meant to build would be an even mightier machine. But she has great weaknesses. She has all the men she wants, these men are by instinct and training soldiers, she has a native talent for organization which is invaluable to a martial nation. But she cannot grow all the food she wants and has bitter memories of the food blockade in the last war. The agricultural states of the Danube valley, however, have all the foodstuffs she needs. Then again, she has not the raw materials she needs; particularly the motor fuel to drive her colossal mechanized armies and air forces. The Danubian States—Rumania, for instance—have many of these things.

How perfect the German military machine would be if these small states could be brought to accept the status of larder and fuel-tank for the great Reich. The thought brings to mind the peace treaty which was imposed on Rumania when she collapsed in the spring of 1918, when the Central Powers seemed on the verge of winning the war. Under this treaty—which the events of six months later overturned—the Rumanians would in perpetuity have laboured in their fields of oil and wheat for the benefit of the Central Powers.

Inevitably Germany and the small Danubian States complement each other economically. Germany is a great industrial country which cannot grow all she needs to eat: the small Danubian States produce foodstuffs in abundance but are backward in industry: the Danube joins them all. It is therefore an inevitable and natural process that the manufactures of Germany should flow down to and dominate the Danubian markets and that their livestock and foodstuffs should flow back. Go to any place on the Danube and you can see it happening. The barge convoys, with the swastika flag, slip swiftly downstream, carrying German tractors and motor-cars and locomotives and farm machinery to Danubia: other barge convoys, laden down to the waterline with grain and fruit and vegetables, toil laboriously upstream to Germany.

v. *The Struggle for Freedom.*

As long as this were a free economic process nobody could say anything against it. But the element of compulsion continually appears in it. Germany to-day cannot pay in freely negotiable cash for her purchases in the Danubian States. She buys enormous quantities of their goods, but pays for them in blocked marks which can only be used to buy German goods. The Danubian States *must* buy German manufactures with them, whether they like it or not, and hence the barge convoys coming downstream with their heavy cargoes of machinery and the like. If they sell to Germany more than they take from her, they do not reap a surplus in cash, but a large book balance in Berlin, which compels them to divert the orders of their own importers to Germany. This already represents a form of dependence, and the line between economic dependence and political dependence is hard to draw. If they received free cash for everything they sold the Danubian States would certainly develop industries of their own. They yearn to, because they have already chosen, whether wisely or foolishly, to follow the West, and they dearly want to make their own silk stockings, their own sewing-machines, their own tooth paste.

After centuries of foreign domination they want to catch up with the West and show that they are as good as any. But the present system compels them to remain tied to agriculture.

What you are witnessing in Danubian Europe to-day, with Czechoslovakia for the key to the whole of the rest of the problem, seems to me an intensely interesting and vastly important struggle. The issue is whether a great historical process which spread over centuries and found its consummation in the World War—the right of the small peoples to liberty—was a just and righteous process, as most people believed until a few years ago, or whether it was wrong, and the World War was fought for nothing or on a false issue, and this process is now to be reversed. How many centuries did it take the small Danubian States, one after another, Hungary, Rumania, Serbia, Greece, Bulgaria, to expel the Turk? How many centuries did it take the Poles and Czechs and Slovaks and Slovenes and Croats to break free of Germanic domination? The process of liberation, though long and painful, then seemed right and inevitable. Is it now to be reversed, the pageant of history made to march backward like one of those trick films where you see racehorses galloping backward to the starting post, or a diver springing back footforemost from the water to the diving-board?

vi. *The Outcome. Watch Czechoslovakia.*

At this moment I do not think any man knows the answer. Up to the annexation of Austria all was clear, for those of us who know Germany. Rearmament, the Rhineland, Austria, all those we foresaw. Now the spotlight has shifted to Czechoslovakia, and none of us can see the outcome. But the question will be answered there, and ,as I think, soon. Will there be war, and what would be the outcome of that war? Will Czechoslovakia ultimately break under the tremendous and prolonged nervous strain and thus clear the way to the rest of Danubia for a process of German penetration that would in form be peaceful, but would only have been possible because of the immense might of Germany? The one thing that seems impossible is that things can long continue as they are. But so many outside factors, some of them a long way off, bear on this problem of Central Europe that a clear forecast on the spot is impossible. The difficulties into which the Japanese seem to have got themselves in China, the unexpected powers of resistance shown by the Republicans in Spain, these far-off factors may act as deterrents on adventurous spirits in Europe. At this moment, when the reserves have been mobilized, there are apparently more men under arms in Germany than at any time since the war. The coming weeks will be anxious ones. But General Winter is on the way: soon the tramp of his advance guard will be heard in the mountains. It is just possible that, if the winter finds Europe at peace, spring will find the balance of forces—now ill-poised because of the laggardliness of the democracies in rearmament—somewhat changed to the disadvantage of the great martial powers. Then, at last, a possibility of stabilization for some years might offer.

It is a small hope, but, as I see it, the only one. In the meantime, watch Czechoslovakia, and you will find there the answer to the political problem of Central Europe.

CHAPTER IV

SOME ECONOMIC EFFECTS OF THE ANSCHLUSS

by

HORACE TAYLOR

Professor of Economics, Columbia University, U.S.A.

i. *Introduction.*

THE annexation of Austria by Germany is a direct fulfilment of an intention stated long ago by Herr Hitler, and maintained as a stable element in the policy of the German Dictatorship. The intention was presented, officially, as a moral obligation of the German nation. Yet mixed with protestations of high ethical purpose has appeared, ever since the close of the World War, a recognition of more tangible economic values which would accrue to Germany through an *Anschluss.* This view of the economic value of Austria was not born in the post-war period or in the mind of Herr Hitler. It had been stated systematically in the *Mitteleuropa* idea of Naumann and others, and was implicit in the still earlier doctrine of Pan-Germanism. An attempt to secure the economic benefits of an *Anschluss,* without entailing the political dangers, was made in the abortive tariff-union negotiations of 1931. At this particular point in time and history, it is interesting to observe a change of values in the German public opinion which—only a few months ago—preached the annexation of Austria as a moral imperative of the Nazi *Weltanschauung.* The same public opinion is now engrossed in a glowing inventory of the material gains that have been made.

The immediate effect of the Anschluss is, of course, that Austria's 84,000 square kilometres of territory and six and one-half million people have been added to Germany's six-times larger territory and ten-times greater population, and that Austria's natural, industrial and human resources have been merged with those of Germany. As a going situation, this means that Austria's resources will be used in conformity with a detailed and inflexible German programme which has preparation for war as its major objective. It means also that the trade which she formerly conducted with other countries will be made subject to German exchange controls and clearing arrangements and that her financial affairs will no longer create business in the capital markets of the world. Without avowing any side in the current conflict of faiths between what is called economic autarchy and what is called economic liberalism, I present these merely as general facts. If they are also obvious facts, I hope that I may be pardoned for roughly surveying the forest before I try to count the trees.

As regards the economic resources which Austria brought into the Greater Reich, they appear at first glance to be similar, rather than complementary, to those of Germany. The proportion of Germany's employed population engaged in industry (41 per cent) was only slightly higher than that of Austria. Some of the principal industries in the two countries produced the same or similar things. Austria, as created by the Treaty of Versailles, fell heir to a large part of the manufacturing capacity which originally supplied the great Austro-Hungarian Empire. It received at the same time a very small share of the old Empire's resources and of its industrially important raw materials. The economic one-sidedness of Austria has been shown, throughout its history, by its exceptionally large per-capita volume of imports and exports. Germany also had to import large quantities of raw materials and foodstuffs and to pay for them by selling her own products abroad. Thus their records definitely show Austria and Germany to have been economically similar rather than complementary. But as regards the economic effects of the *Anschluss,* this is one of those cases—fairly frequent in economics, if not in geometry—in which the whole equals more than the sum of its parts.

ii. *Economic Background of the* Anschluss.

In spite of their economic similarity, Germany has long produced some commodities which Austria needed to buy and Austria has had exportable surpluses of some things badly wanted by Germany. They carried on a considerable trade with each other. Commerce between them would appear, in fact, to have been an obvious result of their contiguity, their common language and traditions, and their respective capacities and needs. But political aims and economic restrictions came to dominate their trade. Differences between the two countries in purpose, in methods and in strength are important in this connection. Commerce between them on a scale which would have made Austria heavily dependent on Germany for certain markets and certain supplies would have been a small drop in the bucket to her ten-times-larger neighbour on the north. This, in the view of the Austrian Government, would give Germany the power of an economic dictator over Austria, which power would eventually be used for political domination. The soundness of this view is strongly attested by the experience of certain other small States of South-eastern Europe which have entered into large-scale commercial relations with Germany.

At any rate the Austrian Government did what it could to find sources of imports and markets for exports in directions other than Germany. This was due in part to the inescapable fact that Austria needed to import some commodities—especially foodstuffs and industrial raw materials—which Germany did not have in quantities sufficient for export. But it also was due in part in Austria's desire to avoid the economic encumbrances and political dangers of carrying on a large volume of trade with Germany. On its positive side, this programme consisted in cultivating favourable trade relations with other countries. The most promising of these was the Rome Protocol of 1934, which aimed at expanding the trade of Austria, Italy and Hungary with each other. Better commercial relations also were fostered with Czecho-Slovakia, Poland, and the Balkan countries. On its negative side, the programme took the form of limitations placed directly on trade with Germany. Due to existing exchange restrictions, for example, it was possible to keep the price of German marks in Austria at an arbitrarily high level. It is reported that this was done to an extent that made it cheaper in some cases for Austrian buyers to purchase German machinery from Swiss dealers than from the German manufacturers.* The late Austrian Government evidently planned to carry the programme still farther. As recently as last February 24th, after his meeting with Herr Hitler at Berchtesgaden, the former Austrian Chancellor,

* Cf. "Economic Consequences of the *Anschluss*," by Arnold Lair, *The Contemporary Review*, July, 1938.

Dr. Schuschnigg, declared : " We are determined to do all in our power to lead our foreign trade out of the wilderness of currency restrictions, clearing agreements and clearing points. . . We lay stress upon further developing our trade intercourse with countries free from a currency control—an intercourse which, in the past year, has been gratifyingly increased by fifty per cent."*

In 1929 Germany's exports to Austria amounted to R.M.441 millions; in 1937 they totalled only R.M.122 million. Even in 1937, 16 per cent of Austria's imports came from Germany. But this marks an important decline from 1929, when one-fourth of her imports were of German origin. The balance of trade between them was consistently favourable to Germany. But the balance of payments, due to invisible items, ran in favour of Austria.†

It has long been argued that Austria was economically incapable of a separate existence. That she could not maintain herself in economic isolation is obvious. But to argue from this that an *Anschluss* with Germany was inevitable involves a fallacy which is equally obvious. Austria's economic accounts certainly were in better order than those of Germany. Her public finances were in stronger position, her currency had a more stable basis, she had balances instead of deficits abroad. One of the long list of recent errors with which Western nations may properly tax themselves is their failure to render more effective economic support to independent Austria. Since

* Chancellor Schuschnigg's address to the Austrian Federal Diet on February 24, 1938.

† These invisible items appear on the balance statements principally as tourists' expenditures and freight-traffic accounts. But an item which some Austrians claimed to be very large and very " invisible " was German subsidies to the Austrian National Socialist Party.

the most direct economic effect of the *Anschluss* has been the obliteration of the late Austrian economy, it will be worth our while to make a brief post-mortem examination of that economy.

iii. *Some Effects on Austria.*

In spite of her economic one-sidedness, in spite of the restrictions implicit in her difficult commercial policy, and in spite of civil disorder and political unrest, Austria achieved striking economic improvements in the period before the *Anschluss*. Both her exports and her imports were higher in 1937 than they had been in any year since 1931. Her unfavourable trade balance of 1937 was lower than that of any year in her history, and was comfortably covered by tourists' expenditures and other invisible payments. Balances held by the Austrian National Bank in foreign banks (amounting to 161 million schillings) were higher than they had been since 1931. By the end of 1937, Austrian foreign debts had been reduced to less than one-half of their 1932 level, and interest costs due to these debts had declined more than proportionately.

Behind these improvements in Austria's international position lay a large increase in her domestic production. Industrial production in 1937 was 23 per cent above the level of 1936 and 6 per cent above that of 1929, the previous best year. Of agricultural commodities—which tend to vary in particular years according to weather conditions—Austrian production had increased steadily and considerably over the preceding several years. Austria's dependence on imports of agricultural goods appear to have been no greater than that of Germany, and, because she started from more meagre beginnings, she had travelled farther along the road toward agricultural self-sufficiency.

The recorded industrial improvement indicates, of course, that Austria participated in the economic recovery enjoyed by most industrial nations during the first six or eight months of 1937. But it also indicates that Austria had sufficient economic virility to be able to take part in this general recovery. And the increase in agricultural production testifies to the success of a long-range plan fostered by the Government of Austria. The gains that were made in production went largely into foreign trade instead of toward increased consumption by the Austrian people. The consumption index of the Austrian *Institut für Konjunkturforschung* inclined downward for several years before the *Anschluss.* And official Austrian unemployment statistics show one worker in four to have been unemployed at the end of last January. Impressive as this proportion is, it is not quite as high as those of Denmark, Norway and Holland for the same point in time and is only slightly higher than that of the United States.*

Rapid economic improvement to Austria in the sense of a larger volume of business and increased employment must inevitably result from the *Anschluss.* That not all of the people in the territory which once was Austria will share in business profits or in jobs may, with this acknowledgment, be left outside the present discussion. The Greater Reich now constitutes one of the largest markets in the world. The trade of the Austrian segment with the other parts of the Reich will no longer be impeded by tariffs and exchange restrictions. Foreign competition cannot interfere with volumes of sales or prices, since

* *Revue Internationale du Travail,* April, 1938.

currency restrictions force Germans to buy at home. In recent months Germany has been handicapped in her economic programme by a shortage of skilled workers, especially in the metallurgical industries. This shortage will mean jobs for those unemployed Austrians who can qualify. The intensive exploitation of Austria's resources in the interests of the German programme will provide employment for many semi-skilled and unskilled workers.

It seems that the Austrians who, as a class, have received the greatest protection from the German authorities in connection with the *Anschluss* are the Aryan capitalists. Their non-Aryan competitors are being removed. Their customary local markets were shielded against the initial impact of competition from the old Reich by the retention of some of the former Austrian tariffs on goods from Germany long after the former German tariffs on goods from Austria had been removed. One of the earliest acts of the German Government following the *Anschluss* was to forbid (except under special conditions) the establishment of Austrian branches by business concerns in the old Reich. In addition to these measures of protection, it is probable that the conversion of Austrian money and Austrian prices into German currency at the ratio of three schillings to two marks caused many Austrian capital claims to be overvalued. Prices and wages may become adjusted at lower levels, but capital claims, being represented by long-time contracts, do not adjust so quickly or so easily.* Lastly, it is clear that employers of labour in Austria now enjoy greater assurance of discipline in their plants and of order in the streets than they have known before.

* Some industrial prices in Austria already have declined.

Whether such economic liberty as they otherwise might have had is too high a price for the immediate gains that individuals and groups may have secured through the *Anschluss* is a question which cannot be answered. Nor can any longer-range balance sheet for Austria be drawn. The people of Austria are launched upon an adventure whose success depends as much upon political chance as upon economic resources and national virtues. If it succeeds, the Austrians may be expected to have a share in the proceeds. If it does not succeed, Austrians will be enmeshed in the collapse of a structure which they had no part in designing and for which the North-German Nazi dictatorship is entirely responsible.

But the German economic programme is itself affected, in important respects, by the annexation of Austria. The German programme aims at the highest possible degree of economic self-sufficiency in peace and in war. The self-sufficiency in peace which is the aim of the programme requires that a large part of the Reich's resources be devoted to preparations for war.

iv. *Austria's Part in the German Programme.*

The most immediate economic gain that the *Anschluss* brought to Germany was the stock of gold and foreign exchange, amounting to 422 million schillings, which was taken over with paper marks by the Reichsbank from the Austrian National Bank. This amount, while not large in relation to Germany's size and needs, was two and one-half times as great as the R.M. 76 million visible balances of gold and foreign exchange held by the Reichsbank. In addition to this, Austria had due at the end of February active "clearing balances" of about 200 million schillings. Cancelling out the 60 million schillings balance due from Germany, the net gain to Germany on this account is more than 140 million schillings.

There also is an uncertain amount of gold, of bank deposits in foreign countries and of foreign securities which, since the *Anschluss,* have been turned over to the Reichsbank by private persons in Austria. No official figures as to the amount of this private sale to the Reichsbank have been given, but estimates run very high. One Austro-German source places the amount of gold at 750 million schillings, of bank deposits at 500 million schillings, and of foreign securities at 500 million schillings.* I believe that these estimates are near enough to the facts for some general conclusions to be drawn. One is that the *Anschluss* brought to Germany an important supply of means for making foreign payments. Another is that this asset to Germany has a present value greater than any possible current liability due to the foreign debts of Austria.†

* "*Osterreich in der grossdeutschen Wirtschaft,*" by S. L. Gabriel, *Jahrbücher für Nationalökonomie und Statistik,* Vol. 147, No. 6, June, 1938.

† In a longer-run sense Austria's foreign debts unquestionably exceed the amount of gold, devisen and foreign securities obtained by Germany through the *Anschluss.* But the German Government already has denied responsibility for the foreign debts of the former Austrian Government, and has made only a reluctant and partial settlement with Great Britain in connection with those loans which were guaranteed by the British Government. Austrian private debts due to foreigners are now subject to exchange restrictions. Thus, as an incidental effect of the *Anschluss,* it appears probable that debts due to foreign creditors will not be paid in full. A possible corollary effect is that Germany may have secured amounts of immediately liquid foreign credits greater than the payment that ultimately will be made to foreign creditors.

Of much greater long-time benefit to the German economy are the supplies of raw materials which Austria produces, or can be made to produce. The most important of these are iron, timber, magnesite, lead and graphite. Of at least equal importance for its potential service to German industry is Austria's enormous endowment of hydro-electric power sites. The only important supply of raw materials that Germany brings to Austria is coal, which was, next to grain, Austria's largest import item in 1937. The raw material accounts of the *Anschluss* seem heavily one-sided, Germany getting much and Austria little. But it is appropriate to bear in mind that Germany's interests are the ones that count. It was not, after all, an Austrian army that invaded Germany last March.

Of the raw materials which have been mentioned, Austria does not produce enough to supply all or even most, of Germany's needs. But she can, and will, be of important assistance to that end. Austria's iron-ore extraction, for example, was 1,800,000 tons in 1937, which is just one-tenth as much as the amount of ore imported by Germany during the same year. But it is virtually certain that Austria's ore extraction can be increased to at least 4,000,000 tons annually. In the famous *Eisenberg* of Styria, Austria possesses literally a mountain of iron-ore. The reserves of ore centreing about this mountain are estimated at from 220 to 350 million tons—which equals only about 10 per cent. of the ore reserves of the old Reich. But the iron deposits of Styria are rich, running about 45 per cent., whereas those of the old Reich do not assay more than 28 per cent. to 33 per cent. The Styrian deposits have the added advantage of running about 3 to 5 per cent. manganese. The current German Four-Year Plan (which, on March 19th, was made to apply to Austria) aims at 50 per cent. self-sufficiency in iron ore by the end of the plan in 1940. The contribution which Austria offers to the attainment of this goal is so large as to make it seem that the iron and steel quotas of the Four-Year Plan must have been drawn in contemplation of the *Anschluss.*

Her shortage of timber has been a major handicap to Germany's economic programme. Austria possesses 7.7 million acres of timber lands, and has been, after Finland and Sweden, the third largest European exporter of timber. Since this timber has been exported from Austria in the form of logs, manufactured lumber and wood pulp, it is difficult to give a total figure for the physical volume of her export. But her timber exports in 1937 were valued at R.M. 88.4 million. Germany's timber imports in 1936 amounted to R.M. 207 million, or about two and one-half times the value of Austrian exports. Austria's principal export to Germany in 1937 was timber and timber products; yet Germany bought only 23 per cent of Austria's total export. In 1937 Austria produced also nearly 30,000 car-loads of paper and cardboard and considerable amounts of cellulose materials. These products testify still further to the importance of Austria's timber resources. These resources can, for some period of time, be made to furnish the old Reich with quantities somewhat in excess of recent Austrian exports.

In addition to her normal needs for wood products, a large part of Germany's production of "*Ersatz*" materials* depends on adequate supplies of raw timber. The embargo which was laid on timber and cellulose, soon after the arrival of German troops in Vienna, testifies to the importance of these materials to the German economy.

Until Russia recently took first place, Austria was the world's largest producer of magnesite. In 1937, she exported 186,000 tons. Although Germany bought 40 per cent. of Austria's export, her purchases from Greece were even larger. Even if Germany continues to buy heavily from Greece on a clearing-agreement basis, the Austrian magnesite will be a highly ventable commodity in those countries which still pay cash for what they buy. Graphite is another material of which Austria is a leading producer and for which there is a fairly active demand in cash markets. Austria's highest annual production—that of 1929—was 25,000 tons. She exported about 90 per cent. of her annual supply, and for this product also Germany was consistently her best customer.

Within the former Austrian territory are a considerable number of lead, zinc and manganese mines which have been, in recent years, principally out of operation. The lead deposits are large, and a few of the mines have remained in fairly steady operation. The extent to which the other minerals can be exploited economically is problematical. In an emergency, however, these Austrian resources may become highly important. This is true also of the considerable Austrian reserves of bauxite, the raw material of aluminium, of which some 3,600 tons were mined in Austria last year. Germany has no bauxite, and,

* As, for example, of synthetic "wool," of which she produced 140,000 tons in 1937.

in an emergency, the Austrian supplies may become crucially important. Austria has large deposits of salt and some coal, in both of which the old Reich has large resources. It is interesting, however, that Austria, while a heavy importer of hard coal, may be able to furnish considerable amounts of lignite to the old Reich. Germany imported lignite to the extent of 600,000 tons in 1937.*

The available water-power resources of Austria can be developed to generate some 25 billion kilowat hours of electrical energy annually. This amounts roughly to one-half of the consumption of electricity by the old Reich. Before the *Anschluss* Austria had developed only a small proportion of her water-power resources. She was, however, an exporter of electrical power to Germany. A rapid exploitation of Austria's hydro-electric resources may be expected. The beginnings of this were indicated in Marshall Göering's announcement, in his speech in Vienna on March 26th, that one billion marks would be used as quickly as possible in developing a power project in Hohen Tauern. In the course of time the use of electrical energy generated in Austria will release workers from some occupations and so help to make available the labour supply needed for some of the expanding phases of the German programme.†

Austria's negative trade balance has been offset, in

* For a complete and excellent summary analysis of Austria's natural resources in relation to the needs of the Greater Reich, see "*Osterreich in der groszdeutschen Wirtschaft,*" by S. L. Gabriel, *Jahrbücher für Nationalökonomie und Statistik,* June, 1938, pages 641-694. I have used some of Dr. Gabriel's figures here, though I have checked them, as far as possible, against their sources or against other estimates.

† For an inventory of Austrian hydro-electric resources, see "*Stromüberschuszland Oesterreich,*" *Frankfurter Zeitung,* March 24th, 1938.

previous years, by invisible items in which tourists' expenditures and transportation receipts have been especially important. Tourists' expenditures probably will be smaller in the immediate future, and revenues from transportation will not be so large, since Germany's payments for these services will no longer appear on the credit side of an Austrian balance of international payments. Transfer of purchases—as, for example, of Polish coal and of Czechoslovakian coal and chemicals—in the direction of the old Reich, should reduce somewhat (though clearly not by the full amount of the transferred purchases) the deficit which Austria appears to present to the international balance sheet of the Greater Reich.

It is in food stuffs that Austria is most deficient, and it is here that her principal liability to the Greater German economy lies. Of grains alone, Austria's per-capita imports have averaged, for the last three years, about five times as great as those of the old Reich. But she had achieved self-sufficiency in potatoes and in sugar. In 1936 and 1937 her export surplus of milk and dairy products averaged more than 200,000 quintals, or about one-sixth of the average amount imported by Germany. And there is reason to believe that Austrian agricultural production can be still further increased.

Germany is famous for its heavy use of artificial fertilizers. In 1937, the amount of nitrogen used per acre of crop land was 13 times as great in Germany as in Austria; the amount of potash used was 16 times as great.* Germany's per-acre yield was higher than that of Austria in wheat by 28 per cent.; rye by 17 per cent.; barley by 21 per cent.; oats by 29 per cent.; potatoes by

* Data showing these proportions from S. L. Gabriel, loc. cit.

18 per cent.; sugar beets by 14 per cent. It may be inferred that it will now be economically feasible to use large quantities of artificial fertilizer in Austria in order to force agricultural yields as they have been forced in the old Reich. And, although Austria has made as much use as possible of *natural* fertilizers, it is probable that the great difference in yields is due largely to differences in the amounts of fertilizer used. If Austrian yields can be raised to the levels reached in the old Reich, Austria will —counting the amounts produced of some commodities in excess of her own needs—come nearer to carrying her own weight as regards these products. In 1937 Austria had an excess of imports of hogs, beef cattle and horses amounting to more than 160 million schillings. She can increase her production of live stock, but she will be limited here by a lack of fodder at economically justified prices. Finally, Austria's deficit in agricultural products may be reduced by restrictions on consumption similar to those now applied to the consumption of fats in the old Reich*

v. *The Real Reason for the Anschluss.*

I hope that I have made clear my grounds for disagreeing with those people who have argued that the annexation of Austria has been of no direct economic advantage to Germany. I wish now to add, however, that I agree completely with the same people when they say that the greatest economic benefit of the *Anschluss* to Germany is the strategic base which Austria affords to the commercial penetration of the Danubian and Balkan countries.

* In this connection it is interesting that Austria's per capita consumption of milk has been about twice that of Germany, and her per capita consumption of butter more than twice as much (8.9 kg. against 3.5 kg. per capita per year).

These territories are the ones on which the trade strategy of the Reich has been most strongly centred since the rise of the Nazi dictatorship. Only a brief outline of that strategy can be presented here.

Since 1933, the year of the Nazi revolution, the volume of Germany's trade with most foreign nations has declined. During this period there have been only six countries with which Germany's trade has increased. These six countries are Hungary, Greece, Bulgaria, Yugo-Slavia, Rumania and Turkey. The volume of Germany's exports to these countries increased from R.M. 191 million in 1933 to R.M. 454 million in 1936; her imports from these countries increased from R.M. 235 million in 1933 to R.M. 504 million in 1936. That is to say, her total volume of trade with these six countries of South-Eastern Europe increased by 125 per cent. in three years. In 1933 Germany's imports from these countries amounted to 6 per cent. of her total imports and exports to them were 4 per cent. of her total exports. These proportions increased, by 1936, to 12 per cent. and 9.5 per cent. respectively. The same figures, translated into proportions of the trade of these commercially small nations, are much more dramatic. By 1937, 25 per cent. of Hungary's total trade was with Germany. In the same relation was 27 per cent. of Yugo-Slavia's, 48 per cent. of Bulgaria's, 24 per cent. of Rumania's, 29 per cent. of Greece's and 39 per cent. of Turkey's. The proportions speak for themselves: What is an increasingly important, but still relatively small, proportion of Germany's foreign trade is, when looked at as a proportion of the trade of each of these six countries, a matter of commercial life or death.

The disparity which has been shown gave Germany

a tremendous power over the economic affairs of these countries, and she has not been loath to use this power. Until the rise of the National Socialist dictatorship, German exports to these countries almost always exceeded her imports from them. More recently, however, the trade currents have been reversed. In the four years, 1933-1936 inclusive, Germany's total imports from these countries have exceeded her total exports to them by almost R.M. 300 million. This balance remains unpaid in the form of block-mark credits in Germany. That is, this amount of money can be used only for the purchase of goods from Germany. Germany has developed her position as debtor to the countries of South-Eastern Europe with such shrewdness that her power, as a debtor, to dictate terms to her creditors is tremendous. She has been able to force her creditors to continue selling to her more than she sells to them, and also to bring pressure on the creditor nations to accept from her the goods that she wants to sell to them at the times that best suit her own convenience. Some of these nations are objecting and resisting, but their ability to do so is limited by their pressing needs. The amount of credit that Germany has forced these comparatively poor countries to extend to her is a heavy burden for them. But the advantage that this method gives to a nation which is feverishingly preparing for war, but which needs food and raw materials in order to carry on these preparations, is obvious. The old theory of empire laid heavy emphasis on investments of capital and loans by the imperialistic power in her colonies. Germany has so reversed the classic doctrine that we are almost justified in paraphrasing to say: "Debtorward the course of empire takes its way."

The formation of the Greater Reich intensifies the economic difficulties of the countries I have mentioned and also those of Czecho-Slovakia and Poland. All of these countries, especially the last two, will be injured by the loss of a part of the trade which they formerly had with Austria. And the part that remains of the trade which they formerly had with Austria will now be subject to the exchange controls and clearing agreements of the Greater Reich. Austria also operated on the basis of clearing agreements with the Balkan countries. But, at the time of the *Anschluss,* her clearing accounts showed credits rather than debits.

To the Greater Reich's programme of economic penetration in the South-East, the former territory of Austria will give an enormous strategic advantage. For Germany, it has an importance almost analagous to that of an outlet to the sea to a previously land-locked nation. Prior to the *Anschluss,* imports to Germany from the Balkan States had to pass through Austria or Hungary or Poland or Czecho-Slovakia, or, in some cases, two of them. To have possible barrier states between herself and her intended sources of food and raw materials is not desirable to a country that is preparing for war. Of course it was inevitable that Germany would, in case of war, occupy Austria and through Austria have access to Hungary and the Balkans. But a much tidier arrangement can be made by being forehanded. Goods can now move over a single German railway system from Hungary, from Yugo-Slavia, or from Italy to the Baltic and intermediate points. And the plan for a canal to join the Danube to the Rhine has been revived. Reverting to my earlier analogy, Vienna serves the same purpose as a seaport to the Greater

Reich. Indeed it is significant that North-German newspapers, since the *Anschluss,* have christened Vienna "the Hamburg of the East."

The several effects of the *Anschluss* which have been discussed in this paper are what economists are accustomed to call "short-time" effects. This is one of those cases, frequent in the larger affairs of nations, in which "long-time" economic effects are determined as much by political trends and by persistent national habits of thought as by more tangible economic conditions. Customary economic analysis breaks down because it is futile to assume that "other things" will "remain equal." Yet broader trend lines can be, and have been, indicated. The one which follows, since it is not my own, is placed in quotation marks: "The subject state will become master if it can and will put no limit on the effort and the sacrifice that the achievement will cost. . . . A map of Europe, which shows the great zone over which, by peaceful penetration, federation, and quasi-annexation, the power of Germany may extend, shows at a glance how insignificant is the domain that Germany has lost in comparison with what she is in a way to gain. It is on the success of this movement—the march eastward and southward of German power under forms of peace—that the whole future of the world depends." This was written by the late Professor John Bates Clark in 1919. The "long-time" economic effect of the *Anschluss* is that it moves along the trend indicated by Professor Clark and brings Germany—and the rest of the world—one step nearer the conclusion which he reached.

CHAPTER V

SPAIN AND THE MEDITERRANEAN

by

IBBETSON JAMES

Geneva Correspondent of the "Daily Herald," "Observer" and Associated Press

THE few remarks for which there is space in this paper should be regarded as a brief essay in Machtpolitik. I shall not be able to do more than touch the fringe of a subject which has occupied statesmen and political philosophers for over three thousand years. All I can possibly do is to indicate what in my opinion is at the moment happening in the inland sea which is still the cradle and centre of world civilisation.

In particular I want to make it clear that, when I use certain phrases in the course of these somewhat random remarks, I do not mean those phrases to be considered as terms of abuse. Thus when I refer, as I shall, to "competing imperialist capitalist groups," I do not want you to assume that I use the word "capitalism" in order to insult capitalists. I use it merely to describe a certain economic organisation of society, an organisation which is comparatively recent and which from the historian's point of view may or may not have "come to stay." When I speak of "Bolshevism" or "the Soviet Republic," I am not trying to be rude. I am using a short phrase for a tremendous social experiment, which is even younger than the social experiment of capitalist imperialism, and which may or may not have "come to stay." When

I use the words "Fascism" or "Nazidom," I am alluding to the economic and political systems which have arisen respectively on the ruins of the World War in Italy and in Germany. The same applies to my use of the adjective "totalitarian." If you do not understand this, what I have to say will have little or no meaning for you, for you will interpret my remarks in the light of your own particular political theories. Let us therefore be clear that I take no sides in what follows.

The Mediterranean is very much "in the news" these days. A distinguished colleague of mine pointed out recently in his paper that it has, since the memory of man, always been "in the news." The Mediterranean has been "in the news" since, three thousand years ago, the ships and armies of the Greek cities of the Aegean launched their concerted attack upon the Dardanelles in rebellion against the intolerable economic domination of Troy. We are told they did this for the bright eyes of a woman. With the best will in the world, we cannot accept the legend. You all know that the Greeks of Homer sailed to the spot which has again been made holy in the twentieth century by the sacrifice of a hundred thousand lives for the purpose of preventing a social unit—the city of Troy—which held the keys of the Dardanelles, from levying excessive tribute upon them. They thus defended their attempts to secure the means of livelihood from the corn-fields of the Black Sea. Three thousand years later, a hundred thousand young men, the flower of a great Empire, were to waste their lives in an attempt to open the way for the supply of munitions to imperialist Russia, then allied with Great Britain and France in a struggle against Germany and Austria-

Hungary. As you all know, the attempt was unsuccessful and the attacking troops were sucked back, " having accomplished nothing but an epic." Because of their failure, and almost entirely because of their failure, the Great Empire of the Czars disappeared in red ruin and slaughter, and post-war Europe assumed the aspect which it assumes to-day. It is not without interest to mention that one of the chief reasons—though there were many for the failure of this second " siege of Troy " was that the imperial régime which the Allied Powers, France and the British Empire, were endeavouring to support, refused to lend any help to the attack on the Dardanelles. Why this decision was made is beyond the scope of what I have to say this morning. Suffice it that imperial Russia made the great refusal, and paid the penalty by ceasing to exist.

I mention this point in advance in order to lead to the situation which existed in the Mediterranean at the end of the World War, 1914-1918. The World War was a struggle centred primarily in Europe, though extending far beyond its bounds, between two groups of imperialist capitalist Powers, which sought to gain for themselves the ultimate and unfettered control of the colonial markets of the world. You all know the result of this war. One group of capitalist Powers, the British Empire and France with the powerful assistance of the United States of America, subdued the other group, and imposed their will upon it. But one of the victorious Powers fell by the wayside. This was the Empire of imperial Russia which, mainly owing to the Dardanelles failure, to which I have referred, could not stay the course and disappeared in the throes of a social revolution. The alignment of world power in 1918 might therefore be described as the alliance of Great Britain and France to hold down the defeated capitalist imperialist group, while on the eastern flank of both appears, for the first time in history, an enormous anti-capitalist dictatorship. This was the problem we had to face in 1919. The history of the Mediterranean in the last twenty years has been largely the effort to react to these problems.

Do not let anyone be surprised that I seem to be going far beyond the bounds of the Mediterranean in what I am saying. Strictly speaking, there is no purely Mediterranean problem. The control of and access to the Mediterranean is bound up with considerations which go far beyond the shores of the inland sea itself. I will make a rough guess and suggest that, from over five hundred miles west of Gibraltar in the west, to the extreme limits of Transjordania and beyond in the east, from the Danube and even from Berlin in the north, to the Equator in the midst of the deserts of Libya and the Sudan in the south, there is no political question which can arise which may not fairly be described as a Mediterranean problem.

i. *Great Britain in the Mediterranean.*

The history of English enterprise in the Mediterranean can be traced back as far as the Third Crusade. From this period there is an increasing, if somewhat sporadic, growth of English trade interests in the Levant, intimately connected with the suppression of the Corsair piracy operating from the African coast. The acquisition of Gibraltar in 1704 was at the outset at least of as much importance as a step on the way to Southern Africa and the Far East *via* the Atlantic, as it was for the protection of British Mediterranean traffic. Later, of course, Gibraltar was to become a *point d'appui* and an arsenal for use against France, in the wars of the 18th century and the wars against the French Revolution and Napoleon. I would draw your attention especially to the importance attached by the British naval authorities in the 18th century to the Balearic Islands. In 1756 a British Admiral was condemned and shot for abandoning the strategical point of Minorca, which lies along the routes of communication from east to west in the Mediterranean.

With the opening of the Suez Canal in 1869, the whole strategical balance in the Mediterranean changes in such a way that Great Britain's interests become paramount. Gibralter, Malta, Alexandria and, later Cyprus and Haifa, become for Great Britain essential for the securing of the trade route between Great Britain, India and the Far East. The forty-year British occupation of Egypt, disguised under the form of securing the due payment of interest to the bondholders of Egyptian loans, is the direct result of the necessity for Great Britain to secure her imperial communications over the new and shorter route.

It has been well said that the British Empire suffers from "curvature of the spine." The immense trade route which stretches from Tilbury and Plymouth through the Bay of Biscay down the Portuguese coast past Gibraltar, through the Mediterranean and the Suez Canal and down the Red Sea, is, at any rate until it reaches the Indian Ocean, intensely vulnerable against an attack by any first-class Power. For many years the dominance of the British Fleet in the English Channel and the Eastern Atlantic, coupled with the fact that there was no first-class Power in the Mediterranean itself, obscured the dangers of this curved spine of the British Empire. The last eighteen years have seriously changed the position.

ii. *The Post-War Mediterranean.*

I previously described the World War, so far as Europe was concerned, as a struggle between two capitalist imperialist groups for the mastery of those portions of the earth which were as yet undeveloped. In that struggle Italy, sitting in the midst of the Mediterranean, athwart British communications, was the ally of the British and French, and moreover could in no way be regarded as a first-class Power. Since the War ended in the victory of the Western Powers, and since heavy terms of peace were imposed upon the defeated nations, there has imperceptibly come a change into the balance of interests of the Powers fringing the Mediterranean. In this connection, four factors must be borne in mind:

1. The fact that France, an under-populated country, draws a very large proportion of the man power of her armies for any European War from her North African colonies, acquired during the 19th century;

2. The fact that the Balearic Islands which, strictly speaking, belong to Spain, lie right athwart these essential communications between France's North African colonies and her southern ports. This fact creates a new factor in the strategic problem in the Mediterranean, a factor which did not exist before the last fifty years; the factor of north to south communications;

3. The fact that Italy, which was on the side of the western capitalist group during the World War has (*a*) abandoned that group for the other group; (*b*) become, under the leadership of an extremely able man, something approaching a first-class Power;

4. The fact that the development of Air Power has completely changed the technical conditions under which any given group of Powers can maintain its supremacy in any given area. This factor has operated entirely in favour of what would previously have been considered the weaker Power, because enormous aerial fleets can be built swiftly and secretly, and do not require the permanent and expensive commitments which are involved in the control of the surface of the sea.

You have here all the elements of a complete reversal of the strategical situation in the Mediterranean.

Add to this other considerations far afield, all of which go to accentuate this change in the Mediterranean balance.

In the first place, the United States, instead of becoming a Member of the League of Nations, founded by the victorious group after the World War, decided to withdraw from international political co-operation.

Secondly, Japan, which acted with the victorious group during the World War, decided to throw in her lot with the other group and, under the pretence of anti-Communism, has been not only absorbing large slices of Eastern Asia, but has been interfering seriously with the trade interests of the victorious group in the Far East. This is a re-orientation of power politics which has produced the situation in the Mediterranean which I will now try to describe.

iii. *The New Situation.*

Certainly for the last three years, and probably for longer, there has been a complete change in the essential Power politics of the Mediterranean. Instead of the dominance of the victorious Powers on the essential trade route, we have the open and increasing threat to that dominance by the members of the other group, re-enforced by a strengthened and bellicose Italy. What we have now —and here I ask you to remember that I speak without taking sides—is the opposition of two new differently orientated imperialist capitalist groups, one of which, represented by what we call the Totalitarian Powers (Germany and Italy), is endeavouring to reverse the defeat inflicted upon Germany in 1918. The other group is represented by what for the sake of shortness we may call the democratic Powers, Great Britain and France. The events of the last three years in the Mediterranean should, I submit, be regarded as a manœuvring for position between these two groups in the event of a further struggle for colonial power. In my view, it would be absurd to deny that in that manœuvring for position the totalitarian States, under their able leaders, Hitler and Mussolini, have completely out-generalled the democratic States. They have been, and are still, endeavouring to secure that, in the event of the struggle which they intend to precipitate at their own given moment, to reverse the Treaty of Versailles, especially as regards its colonial clauses, they should already be in the possession of enormous strategical advantages, advantages which will go far to counter-balance their comparative weakness in military, naval and economic strength.

iv. *The Back Door to Democracy.*

It is clear that, even since 1932, the extremely able rulers of the totalitarian States have been working, each in his own way, to undermine the strength of their possible democratic opponents at any weak link which they can discover. They have acted separately, but with a common aim. To Italy has fallen the task of turning the flank of British communications in the Eastern Mediterranean by securing control of the Empire of Abyssinia. A glance at the map will show you that Signor Mussolini's boast that British influence in Egypt and the Sudan is crushed between the "pincers" of Italian Libya and Italian Abyssinia is no mere idle vaunt. Further north in the East, both the Italians and the Germans have taken astute advantage in Palestine of the fact that the British Government made towards the end of the World War the great political mistake of promising somebody else's property to two totally different sets of people, the Jews and the Arabs. It is not for me to enter in the lamentable history of Palestine under British Mandate, but it is sufficiently clear that the astute politicians of the anti-democratic group have taken full advantage of this Achilles heel of the democratic *entente.*

But such action by no means exhausts the possibilities of the general help which Signor Mussolini has rendered, and can render, to the new anti-democratic group. Signor Mussolini has most astutely "cashed in" on the newly discovered "nuisance value" of Italy as a thorn in the flesh both of democratic France and of the curved spine of the British Empire. Signor Mussolini has deliberately terrified the capitalists of the City of London by threatening them (*a*) with a nation in arms on the imperial route to India and the East; (*b*) with the suggestion that, if they do anything forcible about it, there will be Bolshevism in Italy. As regards Signor Mussolini's second suggestion, no one who knows anything about the Italian nation can possibly imagine that the fall of Mussolini would be followed by Bolshevism in Italy. The whole Italian nation, on the collapse of the Fascist régime, would give a sigh of relief and go back to constitutional monarchy. Unlike developments in Germany, which are outside my province here, there was never any need for Fascism in Italy. That necessity was a pure invention of the genius of Signor Mussolini, and why the great men of the City of London have not called the Duce's bluff is one of the outstanding wonders of the post-War world.

v. *Spain.*

It must be clear that in the struggle for predominance between the two groups, the nodal point is Spain. One of the principal reasons why Great Britain and France weathered the storm of the World War was that they had to deal with a neutral, or at least a non-hostile, Spain. The possession of Spain by their Central European opponents would have been almost a deathblow to that essential control of the Mediterranean upon which so much of their war power depended. Even the neutrality of Spain acted in their favour. The able men who now control the totalitarian Powers are thoroughly aware of this historic fact, and have for the last five years been trying to reverse the situation of the World War. Both for the British Empire and for France, a friendly or neutral Spain is indispensable in the event of a war with some other group of Powers. For Great Britain, whether the British trade route lies through the Mediterranean or outside Spain down the African coast, a friendly or neutral Spain is equally essential. For France the situation is even more serious. The Balearic Islands lie directly athwart the straight route from France's North African Empire to French ports. In the event of a European war, the possession of Majorca by a hostile Power is equivalent to immobilising France's North African mobilisation.

During the World War, France, though threatened from the East, was secure, upon her Alpine and Pyrenean frontiers. As a result of the recent intervention in Spain she is no longer so secure. Her Alpine frontier has become a hostile frontier. It is the intention of the totalitarian Powers that her Pyrenean frontier should equally become a hostile frontier. From the technical point of view, such a development would be equivalent to the immobilisation of a million French soldiers to watch these two hostile frontiers. When you consider the disproportion of population between France and the Reich, this additional handicap for France will appear in its true proportions.

This is the true explanation of the war in Spain. The two groups are manœuvring for position, and it must be confessed that the positions are being won by the totalitarian States.

vi. *Preliminary Manœuvres in Spain.*

As long ago as 1930, or even earlier, Signor Mussolini, with that acute sense of political realities which distinguishes him, had made up his mind that a definite alliance between Italy and Spain was a necessary preliminary for securing the newly-won power of Italy and for blackmailing the British Empire in the Mediterranean. He had hoped to achieve this by an alliance with the then existing dictatorship in Spain. Events in Spain belied his hope, and the advent of the Spanish Republic and the flight of King Alfonso was a severe blow to the totalitarian group. None the less Signor Mussolini continued his policy and the so-called "Spanish Revolution," which broke out in July, 1936, is now known to have been planned in Rome as early as March, 1934. On that date the representatives of the Monarchist and anti-Republican groups in Spain held a secret meeting with Signor Mussolini and with Marshal Balbo. The document which was the result of their deliberations is now public property. I read you the following extract from it:

> "The undersigned, . . . hereby confirm the meeting held at 4 p.m. to-day, March 31st, 1934, with the chief of the Italian Government, Signor Mussolini, and with Signor Italo Balbo.
>
> "The Duce, after receiving detailed replies to his many questions concerning the present political situation in Spain, and the aspirations of the Army and of the Monarchist parties, stated as follows:
>
> 1. That he is willing to lend material assistance to the parties opposed to the present Spanish régime, for the purpose of overthrowing it and establishing a regency to prepare for the complete restoration of the monarchy.
>
> 2. That to prove his good intentions, he is willing to let us have immediately 20,000 rifles, 20,000 hand-grenades, 200 machine-guns, and, in cash, 1,500,000 pesetas.
>
> 3. That such aid will be in the nature of initial assistance, and will be supplemented by more substantial help if and when circumstances make it necessary."

Signor Mussolini was better than his word of 1934, and Italian re-enforcements in the shape of "volunteer" troops, airmen, and technical assistants, have been poured into Spain in the last two years.

Herr Hitler has not been behindhand. After two years of civil war in Spain, there are at least ten thousand Germans fighting for General Franco, nearly all of them in key positions. The object of both Powers of the totalitarian group is the same. It is not the destruction of "Bolshevism." It is the strategical control of Spain for the forthcoming war. The Air Forces and the artillery experts of the two totalitarian Powers are engaged in transforming Spain into an armed camp hostile to France on the north and to Great Britain on the side of Gibraltar. Italy effectively occupies Majorca. I remember a conversation which I had the other day with a good Spanish friend of mine who is a supporter of General Franco. He outlined for me the argument that, when he had won his war, General Franco would dismiss his German and Italian friends and turn to the other capitalist group, from which alone he could hope to secure the necessary credits for developing the country which he had conquered. I asked him, what General Franco would do if, for example, his Italian friends refuse to evacuate Majorca. I pointed out that, with the best will in the world, General Franco had not got a navy, and Signor Mussolini had. "In that case," he said, "the British will recover Majorca for us."

I do not think any comment is necessary.

In fact, the leaders of the totalitarian Powers are thoroughly alive to the famous dictum of Bismarck: "Put the Spanish fly on France's back."

The French General Staff is quite aware of the

danger. I need only quote the following extract, written recently in a great British daily, by *Pertinax,* the famous French foreign correspondent:

"After two years of activity in Spain, Italy and Germany are now in a position to hamper and delay at will the mobilisation of the French Army by their hold upon Majorca, Spanish Morocco and the Spanish seaboard.

"That danger was fully perceived on March 16th, when the Council of National Defence (which consists of the leading Ministers and the Chiefs of the General Staff for the Army, the Navy and the Air Forces) met to examine the precautionary steps that ought to be taken if France were to be called on to carry out her obligations towards Czechoslovakia.

"The ministry of Foreign Affairs and the higher command are at one in thinking that, as soon as possible, an end must be put to that dislocation of the accustomed strategic equilibrium in the Middle Sea. The military authorities in Northern Africa are even afraid lest, in an emergency, a few Spanish divisions, led by German and Italian officers, should be thrown into Morocco to provoke a rising against the French Protectorate."

Similar views were expressed recently by Mr. Winston Churchill:

"The Germans have not fought in the field, but their highly competent technical assistance has permeated every part of the Nationalist system and administration. They possess a very powerful and efficient Air Force in Spain. Their airfields lie within striking distance of the munition establishments of Southern France. At any moment they can treat the great city of Toulouse as they have treated Barcelona.

"They will be directed from Berlin in accordance with the general plan of Nazi expansion and, of course, in relation to any approaching war.

"It would be natural for them to seek to impose upon

General Franco and the forces which he disposes the Nazi system and characteristics, and in this the Phalangists will be their instruments.

"A thoroughly Nazified Spain, retaining its German nucleus, may well be a cause of profound anxiety both to France and Britain. At any rate, it appears to be a matter upon which they should exert themselves, if indeed the faculty of action still resides among them."

But I would not wish to give you merely quotations from the representatives of one of the two competing groups. Let me quote from a lecture delivered in the spring of this year by Professor Max Gruen, the well known German geologist, who delivered the lecture immediately after a visit to Signor Mussolini in Italy. Professor Gruen entirely corroborates the view of the spokesmen of the democratic Powers as concerns the designs of the totalitarian Powers in Spain. I quote his own words:

"The war in Spain is a European war that is being waged for supremacy (*Vorherrschaft*) in the Mediterranean," said the Professor. "Hitherto Italy has played the part of a power submissive to England and France—for example, in the World War. But the strength she has now achieved, as well as her geographical position allows her to pursue an active policy.

"To-day Italy is England's strongest rival in the Mediterranean. *If Spain falls into the hands of Franco, then Gibraltar is threatened, and the transport of French troops from the colonies will be made almost impossible because of the fortified Balearic islands. When this has happened, Germany WILL PLAY HELL ('Rollschuh fahren') with France in a way that country has never experienced throughout the whole of her history.*

"France has girded herself with concrete armour along her eastern frontier, but she forgot that her Italian sister would abandon her one day. 'Marianne' is vulnerable on the Italian frontier: 600,000 Italian troops are ready to invade France in case of need.

"The Sudan is embraced by an Italian pincer-formation . . . The Suez Canal is threatened by Italy to-day. The Mosul-Haifa oil pipe-line can be destroyed with the help of the Arabs in case of emergency, so that the English Mediterranean fleet will be deprived of its oil reserve.

"Japan may be counted on to use the opportunity of seizing Hong-Kong, and thereby as good as excluding England from the Far East. England will have to swallow whatever (*den Knodel schluken*) Germany and Italy set before her. The whole world is laughing at England in her impotence to-day. She would not have put up with this before 1914. England is trying to overtake Germany and Italy by means of her tremendous rearmament. But we are too far ahead with our armaments to be overtaken. The days of the Halifaxes are over. We demand what was stolen from us—our colonies. In case of war, Italy will annex part of Southern France."

vii. *The Present Issue.*

Such, as I have tried to give it you from both angles, is the strategical situation in the Mediterranean to-day. The totalitarian group have every prospect of securing Spain as a *point d'appui* for their attack upon the democratic group. They have secured not only most of the Iberian Peninsula, but the Balearic Islands. They already possessed, through the emergence of Italy as something approaching a first-class military Power, the possibility of seriously interfering with vital British and French communications in the Mediterranean. In addition, disturbances in the Far East, the possible neutrality of the United States, and the evident unwillingness of large sections of the population of the democratic Powers to collaborate with what they call "Bolshevism," have all acted as additional factors militating, for the time being, in favour of the totalitarians. A further point—though it is strictly speaking outside my province—is that Germany's conquest of Austria has at any rate opened the way to an attack down the Danube upon the democratic Powers' control of the eastern section of the inland sea. With the victory of General Franco in Spain, a victory which the totalitarian group ardently desire, and which the democratic group only half-heartedly resist, the stage is set for a new capitalist imperialist death-struggle in the Mediterranean.

No man can honestly claim to foresee the outcome of this alignment of forces. The issue depends upon too many imponderables, such as developments in the Far East, or the ultimate attitude of the United States in the event of one European capitalist group fighting the other for power. But one thing is clear, that there is now—thanks mainly to the policies of the British and French Governments during the last eighteen years, no consideration whatsoever, except that of self-interest, which can deter one of the two groups from letting loose war upon the other. The British and French Governments, which might have made, even of the imperfect instrument of the League of Nations set up at Versailles, an organisation for world conciliation, have preferred to retain that organisation as an instrument for perpetuating the injustices of the peace which followed the triumph in 1918 of one capitalist group over the other. It is possible that they may now reap the whirlwind.

If this new calamity comes upon us, no one can foretell the issue. The totalitarian States may collapse under the over-prolonged burden of a task beyond their economic strength. On the other hand, the severe handicaps, especially of a strategical nature, imposed in advance upon the European democracies, particularly as the result of the war in Spain, may make it impossible for them to retain their colonial empires against the thrust of the totalitarians. One thing, however, is certain, that the death-grapple in the Mediterranean, if and when it comes, will be the end of all for which Mediterranean civilisation has hitherto stood. The balance of real power will shift finally, as it has already partially shifted—for real power follows real prosperity—to the western coasts of the Atlantic, and on the shores of the once proud Mediterranean there will exist no more than a few agglomerations of impoverished and de-civilised fishermen, wringing a precarious living, amid the shattered monuments of their past glories, from the inland sea whose civilisation their ancestors wantonly destroyed.

CHAPTER VI

FRENCH POLICY AND CURRENTS OF FRENCH OPINION

by

ALEXANDER WERTH

Paris Correspondent of the "Manchester Guardian" and author of "The Destiny of France," etc.

i. *The Main Problems of French Foreign Policy.*

THERE are some who say that there is no such thing as French foreign policy since it is nothing more than an obedient reflection of British foreign policy. A friend of mine in Paris said to me at the time of the Royal visit last month: "This visit crowns the Anglo-French entente; and is it not truly symbolic that their Majesties should, of all places, have taken up their residence at the Quai d'Orsay?"

Personally, I do not think this is quite true. Though French and British policy have, in a large measure, been "co-ordinated" in the past two years, France has not always looked either at Spain or at Czechoslovakia through British eyes. The French have, on occasions, been guilty of deviations—to use the Soviet phrase—from the General British line; and once or twice they have attempted to take the lead; and Britain has followed, at least for a short time.

So French foreign policy cannot, I think, be dismissed as being merely a copy of British foreign policy. I cannot deal here with all the aspects of so big a subject and shall confine myself to the three most salient problems —Spain, Franco-Italian relations, and Czechoslovakia.

ii. *Spain.*

Spain has in the last two years been one of the most vital issues not only in French foreign policy, but also in French home politics. The country was sharply divided on this issue from the outset, and, what is even stranger, it has remained divided on it, even after it had become clear that Italian and German intervention in the Spanish war was ultimately directed against France, and France's most vital interests.

I shall not here go into the details of how the policy of non-intervention was decided upon. In my book, *The Destiny of France,* I have shown how Blum proposed non-intervention under British pressure; a pressure which, however (it is only fair to add), was willingly accepted, not to say, welcomed, by M. Delbos and other Radical members of the Blum Cabinet. The Front Populaire was then in its heyday, and Blum, who was still expecting wonders from it, was not prepared to break it up; and the Spanish Republic was sacrificed on the altar of French Front Populaire "solidarity." Mr. Eden has frequently denied this British pressure on the French Government and has disclaimed responsibility for the *unilateral* non-intervention on which France decided on the 8th of August—a grave step which Blum afterwards attributed to his own desire to show Italy and Germany a noble example, and to "pique their honour"! Nevertheless I maintain that such pressure *was* exercised on the French by the British Ambassador in Paris, what ever may have been the latter's official instructions from London. It is true that three weeks later Italy and Germany subscribed to the non-intervention principle; but they never ceased to violate it. They have equipped and organised Franco, they have sent him about 100,000 "volunteers"; their aeroplanes have killed thousands of civilians and women and children; and their experiment in high explosive bombing in Barcelona last March and April provided the world with a charming foretaste of the totalitarian war which we may, or may not, avoid. And the purpose of it all is not to "stamp out Bolshevism," but to extend the Berlin-Rome axis to Spain; to make Spain a stronghold of Fascism, and one with the help of which France will be encircled by Fascist Powers and her sea route to North Africa cut off, and England's access to the Mediterranean severely threatened. I do not say that Spain will necessarily become, after a Franco victory—if it comes—a base for military operations against France and England—but it will be a tremendous instrument of blackmail against the two Western Democracies. For it still remains to be proved that the ultimate objectives of Rome and Berlin are different; and that by marching into Austria, Berlin has already cracked the Axis. The hope that, in the long run, the Axis cannot work, can, at its best, be only a reckless gamble. And Mr. Chamberlain's policy is essentially a gamble.

He is also gambling on the hope that when Franco wins the war he will get rid of his Italian and German allies. Both Mr. Chamberlain and Mr. Eden have said that, *in the long run,* Spain will never tolerate foreign domination. Maybe, but what matters is not the long run, but the short run. I daresay, Spain will be Spanish in the year 2000; but will she be purely Spanish in a military and political sense during the vital and critical years of 1939 and 1940? Is it certain that a victorious Franco will eat out of our hand, and turn out his Germans and Italians just for the sake of a Reconstruction Loan in the City of London?

What has been France's attitude to Spain all along? Has she or has she not (as is being constantly proclaimed in the German and Italian press) failed to observe the non-intervention agreement? On the whole, she has observed the agreement and with lamentable results to herself. Certain quantities of armaments have, of course, reached Spain from France and via France. But one must distinguish between several things. In the first few months of the war Left-Wing opinion in France felt so strongly about Spain that a considerable amount of ammunition continued to be privately shipped to the Government side; I emphasise the word "privately"; for the private enterprise of the working class organisations in smuggling odds and ends into Spain was inevitably limited in scope and had constantly to reckon with obstruction by the Government. As for Franco he was getting his aid direct from the Fascist Governments—an enormous difference. And the obstruction by the French Government was increased by the everlasting denunciations of such clandestine shipments in the French Right-Wing press. These denunciations (many of which, by the way, were false) played, needless to say, into the hands of Germany and Italy, which never ceased to reproduce under gigantic headlines these "revelations" and "denunciations" from the four, the Action Française, Candide and Gringoire.

But whatever may have been smuggled into Spain in

the last months of 1936, it is certain that throughout almost the whole of 1937, while German bombers were destroying Gernika and flying in large numbers over France to join Franco's forces, the French frontier into Spain was as good as hermetically sealed to armaments. During the greater part of that year an international control commission was working on the Pyrenees frontier; and it worked extremely efficiently, and Captain Lunn the head of this control paid, you will remember, the warmest tributes to the loyal co-operation of the Gardes Mobiles. I remember going down to the Ariège and the Pyrénées Orientales last summer and making a careful investigation on the spot; the control was as effective as it could possibly be. The control inspectors—who, I may add, included a good number of violent "anti-Reds"—were doing their job thoroughly; and I have strong reason to believe that there was nothing like it on the Portuguese border, where, incidentally, nearly all, if not all, of the British Control inspectors—most of them residents in Lisbon—were Pro-Fascist. Then there was the sea; the Rebels were getting uninterrupted supplies by sea. As for the Government they also were getting supplies by sea, but these were almost completely interrupted for a time by the piracy in the Mediterranean—a piracy to which an end was put only by the Nyon agreement. This agreement was the only genuine achievement of "democratic" diplomacy during the whole of 1937. It was largely the work of M. Litvinoff and may I add, of Mr. Eden at his very best —for Nyon was one of the rare occasions when Mr. Eden succeeded in shaking off the fetters of Downing Street. In the circumstances M. Delbos boldly followed.

M. Litvinoff worked hard; for he knew that the continuation of piracy would mean the end of the Spanish Government. I was in Madrid last December and I may say that if the prestige of the Communists was very high then, it was owing to the realisation that Russia had at least done her best to counteract, as much as possible, the systematic violations of non-intervention by Germany and Italy. Unlike France and England, Russia had refused to close her eyes and say, as MM. Blum and Delbos and Mr. Eden and Mr. Chamberlain were saying, that "Non-intervention was a good thing in itself." One may candidly say that but for what might be called Russia's "counter-violations" of the Non-intervention Agreement, this agreement would have been nothing but an instrument for the deliberate massacre and strangulation of the Spanish Republic. But Russia was alone, and far away, and Germany and Italy were closer at hand; and that is largely why, on balance, the Government has been losing ground ever since the war began.

It is true that towards the end of 1937 the French frontier control relaxed somewhat after the international frontier control had been suspended. At the time of the Teruel offensive, substantial amounts of war material were allowed to reach Spain—mostly from Czechoslovakia; and the frontier control was further relaxed at the end of March, when M. Paul Boncour became Foreign Minister in the short-lived Blum Government. It may be added that, by that time Russian shipment had, for various reasons, diminished, one of them being perhaps the growing demands made on Russia by the Chinese Government. March and April, it should be remembered, were the blackest months in the history of the Spanish Republic. The Rebels had reached the Mediterranean and, after the terrible bombings of Barcelona, it looked as though the Government's nerve might easily give way.

It was precisely at this time that Mr. Chamberlain concluded his agreement with Italy; and this agreement, as he himself openly admitted, was partly based on the expectation of a rapid Franco victory.

The relaxation of the French frontier control during these two months was, if not of decisive, at any rate of considerable importance in helping the Spanish Government to pull itself together after the debacle of the Aragon Front. And now the war is going on, with a smashing Franco victory looking certainly much more remote than it did three months ago.

iii. *French Public Opinion on the Spanish War.*

Before I deal with the latest developments in French policy in relation to Spain, I should like to say something about the strange currents of French opinion in relation to the Spanish civil war: for amazing as it may seem, a considerable proportion of French opinion is still pro-Franco. The thing was conceivable at first when the war seemed—though it never was—a purely Spanish affair. (You may remember that on July 29th, ten days after the war had started, a number of Italian bombers crashed in Algeria on their way to Spanish Morocco. So there is not the slightest doubt who "started" intervention.) But it does seem extraordinary that even to-day, and ever since Italy and Germany openly intervened in Spain with the clear, or at any rate, highly probable object of stabbing France in the back some day, so many Frenchmen should still be pro-Franco. At first, no doubt, they loved Franco because Franco meant a reaction against the Spanish

Front Populaire, or the Frente Crapular, as the senile General de Castelnau so wittily put it in the *Echo de Paris* some time in August, 1936. France was then in the heyday of the Front Populaire; the French bourgeoisie had become thoroughly scared of the stay-in strikes and of the "Reds" in general; and if the extermination of Reds had begun in Spain, why, it might somehow start in France, too! It was not very clear how—but still, the prospect was highly pleasing to the French *bien pensants.* Actually, the Cagoulard affair was in a large measure determined by a desire on the part of certain French interests to "play Franco" in France—even if it meant doing it with the help of foreign Fascist countries. But even without being Cagoulards, many Frenchmen felt, and continue to feel, that "since Franco is against the Left, he must be a good man."

To quote a curious English parellel of this sentiment, I remember asking a British general to tell me quite candidly whose victory in Spain would be preferable from the point of view of the British Empire, and from a naval and military point of view. "I am asking you," I said, "a strictly technical question." He reflected for a moment and then said, "Franco." "Franco, why?" I said. "Because," he said—and his answer was sublime—"because I hate the blooming Bolsheviks." And that was a technical answer to a technical question. The same sort of thing is to be found in France; you will forgive me if I read to you a few extracts from a French Ode to Franco called "*The Crusader,*" published in a paper called *Occident.* Now *Occident* is admittedly a Franco propaganda sheet; but I cannot and will not believe that a poem like this could have been written to order.

It is a pathological document, and such a specimen of French female hysteria cannot have been produced simply in order to make a couple of hundred francs. Here goes:

> " Every morning the Silent man
> rises early and goes to morning Mass.
> On his shoulders rests the whole
> weight of western civilisation.
> The man whom God has chosen
> now kneels to the Living God
> and says his prayers.
> It is he who will save the France
> of St. Louis, and of Joan of Arc . . .
> Oh thou who art chosen by God to
> be a rampart of hope and faith
> against the Powers of Hell,
> Let an unknown woman say to you
> softly—Thank you, thank you for
> God and thank you for France.

A large part of the Paris press, if not quite so hysterical, is often nearly so. I remember a story in the *Action Française* of how the Pasionaria bit through the throat of a poor old monk in the streets of Madrid till he was dead.

It must be said, however, that certain elements even of the Right have lately become very uneasy about Franco.

Kerillis, for instance, though pro-Franco on general grounds, is now profoundly disturbed by the hold Italy and Germany have taken over him; Franco is, in consequence, becoming a menace to France. " If only," he says plaintively, " we had backed him from the start, instead of supporting the Reds, think what a difference it would have made to France." Such lamentations, without being based on anything practical (for how was

France going to " back " Franco, who was already being backed by Italy and Germany?) have nevertheless a certain logic. " Franco might have been our friend, but now he is our enemy."

More remarkable still have been the sharp reactions against Franco among some of the French catholics—on both political and religious grounds. They are feeling profoundly uneasy about Franco, who has been massacring women and children and civilians by the thousand, but who nevertheless continues to proclaim himself—just as the above poem calls him—a Crusader, a Soldier of Christ. M. François Mauriac, the famous Catholic writer, has written some remarkable articles on the subject in the *Figaro*; and probably the most important piece of political writing that this century has produced is Georges Bernanos' "*Les Grands Cimetières Sous la Lune.*" It is a merciless analysis of the pseudo-Christianity of the Spanish rebels, and the most powerful denunciation that has ever been made of the middle-class Frenchman's Mussolini-worship and Franco-worship :

> " I should never have spoken of General Franco," he says, " if you had not tried to turn a sort of nightmare Galiffet into a Christian hero."

I know French Catholics who, bitten by the Fascist bug, are unwilling to admit the growing breach between the Vatican and Fascism, and who were made extremely angry by Bernanos's overwhelming book and who have dismissed him contemptuously as a " Dominican," but, on the whole, the French Church is socially and humanely minded; and is largely in sympathy with the Bernanos-Mauriac point of view.

iv. *The Attitude of the French Government to the Spanish War.*

Now, to return to the attitude of the French Government towards the Spanish war. As distinct from certain members of the British Government, the French Governments of the last two years have not desired a Franco victory, though few of them have done much to stop it.

An interesting state of affairs arose in May of this year. Under the short-lived Blum Government, M. Paul Boncour, the Foreign Minister, had done his best to relax the frontier control, and had so rendered the Spanish Government a considerable service at a particularly critical moment. What was the position when the Daladier Government came into office? M. Daladier himself, under the influence of his military advisers, and personally with few illusions about a friendly Italy or a friendly Franco-Spain, was inclined to be in favour of supporting the Spanish Government by keeping the frontier control " relaxed." But it so happened that just about that time the Anglo-Italian agreement was signed. In spite of innumerable past disappointments, French illusions as to the possibility of coming to terms with Italy and—needless to say—of driving a wedge between Rome and Berlin die hard; and in May there was a loud clamour in the press for a *rapprochement* with Italy. M. Bonnet, who, many of you will remember, ate such humble pie in the company of Lord Halifax over the Abyssinian affair at the Council Session in May, felt that no sacrifice was too great to " win over " Italy; and he was ready to help to strangle the Spanish Government by closing the frontier at that critical moment. He was genuinely afraid of a German attack on Czechoslovakia—it was just before the 21st of May. Then, however, came the Geneva speech, in which Mussolini said that "France and Italy were fighting on different sides of the barricade." The speech was so violent in its treatment of France, that even with a minimum of self-respect France could not very well respond to it by closing completely the Catalan frontier. And then came the 21st of May, which showed that Anglo-French firmness could succeed even in the face of a combined Italo-German "threat"; for there is little doubt that the menacing Genoa speech of May 18th was part and parcel of the German offensive against Czechoslovakia. In any case the Spanish policy of M. Daladier prevailed on that occasion over the more defeatist policy of M. Georges Bonnet.

It was not until two or three weeks later, when Mr. Chamberlain's hopes of a rapid Franco victory had been shattered, that the British Government again took up the old scheme for the withdrawal of "volunteers." The French were then "persuaded" to close the Catalan frontier to armaments; Mr. Chamberlain said that the decision had been taken by the French "independently," but his phrase was a quibble. The French would certainly not have taken the decision on their own initiative, though they took it "independently" in a strictly technical sense. The purpose of this decision was apparently to put Italy and Germany in a good mood for entering into the new negotiations regarding the withdrawal of "volunteers." What good this new and almost quixotic demonstration of French "goodwill" has done is not clear. The closing of the frontier was accepted as a new sign of weakness; and the withdrawal scheme is no more advanced than it was two months or ten months ago. The French have now probably opened up the frontier again to some extent, but secretly, as though they were committing a shameful offence, for they still fear to "annoy" and "provoke" Italy and Germany. As if the closing of the frontier on June 14th had improved Franco-Italian relations by one whit!

Franco-Italian relations are now worse than they have ever been; and all the French cringing to Italy has been in vain. Everybody in France, even the Left, desires friendly relations with Italy; but Italy's attitude has lately become such that the French Government has largely come to the conclusion that Italy is not worth bothering about any longer. If a war with Germany is inevitable, then, and no sooner, will the time be ripe for talking to Italy—then, and only then, will there be a chance of really talking business to her. Until then all talks with Italy will provide her merely with new occasions for blackmail. Let matters drift—let us see how the Berlin-Rome axis works in practice—that is, roughly the present attitude of the French Government. The lesson learned by Mr. Chamberlain that no gentlemen's agreements with Mussolini are of the slightest practical value has also been learned by the French Government. Even the Mussolini-worshipping press of the Right is disappointed in Italy; and speaks of her bitterly; though more in sorrow than in anger. With a remarkable lack of dignity the "Temps" continually reminds Italy that it was largely thanks to France that the sanctions experiment failed, and that she does not deserve such unkind words from Italy—as, for instance, those of the Genoa speech. And the French papers go on sighing for a new Stresa—

 H

even though they should know perfectly well that Stresa was nothing more than a conference at which Mussolini bamboozled England and France into giving him a free hand in Abyssinia.

v. *The Attitude of France and Czechoslovakia.*

It remains for me to say something about French policy in relation to Czechoslovakia. Until the 7th March, 1936, when the German army reoccupied the Rhineland and tore up Locarno (an action which received wild applause from large sections of British opinion who completely failed to realise that it meant, perhaps, a death blow to collective security) until that time the Franco-Czech alliance was taken for granted; it was never questioned. Officially, it was never questioned afterwards either; but the mere fact that the Blum Government and the two Chautemps Governments and the second Blum Government and now the Daladier Government have from time to time felt obliged to renew their assurances to Czechoslovakia shows in itself that there was some doubt in various quarters whether France would carry out her obligations if and when it came to the point. Certain organs of the British press had clearly stated that England was not interested in Czechoslovakia; and towards the end of 1937 some articles and speeches suggesting that France was not much interested either began to be published in France too.

It was obvious ever since the 7th March, 1937, that collective security, which had already suffered so severe a blow through the Hoare-Laval plan, would now have a serious technical obstacle placed in its way, in the shape of the German Rhineland fortifications. While the

Rhineland was demilitarised it was obviously easier for France to come to the assistance of the Czechs than it was going to be now. Not that fortifications are in the end decisive, for even with the present fortifications in the Rhineland France can still make war on Germany—for war to-day is not merely a question of military technique, but a thing with a hundred different aspects—Germany can be beaten by a coalition, a blockade or a war of exhaustion.

Now, the deterioration of the French system of alliances, the disintegration of the League, the new obstacle placed by the remilitarisation of the Rhineland in the way of collective security, all of which has resulted in the relative increase of Germany's armed power and the diminution of France's—this disintegration of the French system of alliances became singularly apparent during M. Delbos' tour in Eastern Europe, when he went to Warsaw, Bucarest, Belgrade and Prague. With the exception of Prague, all the other allies and friends of France had become rather lukewarm. At Belgrade an incident occurred which prompted my friend, Dell*, to say "Anyone who cried 'Vive la France' was shot down by the police"! You remember that a crowd of demonstrators at Belgrade who were shouting "Vive la France!" were actually fired on. No doubt they were at least as much anti-Styadinovitch as they were pro-French; but still it was awkward; and it rather emphasised the fact that whatever certain sections of Jugoslav opinion felt about France, the Government was not pro-French.

Delbos returned to Paris in a very gloomy mood. And it was about this time that M. Flandin suddenly came

* Geneva Correspondent of the *Manchester Guardian.*

forward with his defeatist arguments to the effect that France should drop Central Europe, entrench herself behind the Maginot line and try to become an Empire Power; in short, that she should try to imitate the British Empire. This would be perfect; only M. Flandin found some difficulty in convincing his public that either Italy or Germany would in the long run *allow* France to be a great Empire Power—Mussolini wants the Mediterranean, and Hitler, after achieving hegemony in Eastern Europe, desires the destruction, the *Vernichtung* of France; and nothing would be easier for the two dictators than to destroy France, once Germany had become all-powerful through her conquest of Central and Eastern Europe. M. Flandin nevertheless persisted; and a moment came when he suddenly began to feel as though he had become the Man of the Future—that was when Mr. Eden resigned.

Now, M. Flandin, in my opinion, is not a political problem at all, but a personal problem, I might almost say a psychological problem. He is a person who, even when he was premier in 1934, never succeeded in making an impression. He lacks personality; he lacks something; he is an intelligent parliamentary debater and yet a monumental bore. In 1935 while he was Foreign Minister, he was completely eclipsed by Laval who, with all his faults, had a rather magnetic personality. In 1936, when he was Foreign Minister in the ill-fated Sarraut Cabinet, he made the most lamentable performance you could imagine. During the League Council in London that followed the violation of Locarno, he cried and wept. That League Council, you will remember, was a complete getaway for Hitler. And yet now, M. Flandin announces with the most grandiloquent airs that it was he who brought about the Anglo-French Entente of March, 1936. An arrogant and totally unjustified claim; the British guarantee to France and Belgium was (as was quite inevitable) proclaimed by Mr. Eden in the House of Commons on March 9—and this guarantee would have been proclaimed whoever was Foreign Minister in France. M. Flandin had mighty little to do with it. Another episode during that tenure of office as Foreign Minister, an episode of which M. Flandin does not like to be reminded, was his sponsorship of the Franco-Soviet Pact.

Well, to cut the story short, M. Flandin thought that, with Mr. Eden's resignation his chance of being a great man had suddenly come. He proceeded to impersonate Mr. Chamberlain and the "new policy." But Flandin has not even the courage of his convictions—or the courage of his lack of convictions. For I do not believe for a moment that Flandin believes what he preaches; he wants to create an impression, and when he fails to create one, he climbs down, and says that he has been misunderstood. His speech in the Chamber on February 26, for instance, was a complete climb-down. And yet after a time he turns on the same old record again—retrenchment behind the Maginot Line and all that. In a way, I think he is also trying to play a curious party game; to rally round himself both the pro-Fascist and the defeatist elements in France. Only in a parliamentary sense, the campaign is of no importance. For who says, like M. Flandin, "To Hell with Czechoslovakia"? Very few people say it, though a certain number believe it, and a number of papers, some of them directly subsidised by Germany, have said so. But the Right is by no means united on this question; far from it. Louis Marin is essentially anti-German; and so is the greater part of his group; they are people brought up in the Poincaré and Barrès tradition. There may be, on the other hand, some rural village pump radicals and even socialists who, at heart, are in agreement with Flandin—" to Hell with Czechoslovakia." But there is no other point of contact between them and the pro-Fascist elements on the Right—and there is therefore no basis for any sort of political co-operation between them. M. Flandin's idea of becoming leader of the opposition and eventually Premier, on the basis of his defeatest foreign policy therefore falls to the ground.

He cannot even claim any longer to " represent the British Government." For it should be said—and the point has perhaps been overlooked by those who think that Chamberlain is all black (for sometimes he is dark grey) that there is not one Chamberlain policy, but two Chamberlain policies—particularly in relation to France and Central Europe.

The first was that which Mr. Chamberlain proclaimed immediately after Eden's resignation. It *was* a policy of sheer defeatism. " Small and weak nations must not delude themselves into believing that they can rely on any help against aggression." You remember the famous passage from his speech of February 22nd—a passage which was like balm to the soul of Hitler as he was preparing to march on Vienna.

After the *Anschluss* Chamberlain ceased to speak in defeatist terms. Why? Partly perhaps because he realised what immense damage in Central Europe had already been done by his speech of February 22nd, and partly because the French were becoming desperate. Paul

Boncour actually attempted a rather different policy from the British apron-string policy and it is only fair to say that M. Delbos dissociated himself for once from Great Britain when, after Eden's resignation and Chamberlain's speech, he repeated that France's policy was "unchanged."

Paul Boncour attempted a belated return to what is called the Encirclement policy of Barthou and the emphasis was this time no more on the British Entente; France, he thought, would attempt a somewhat more independent policy with an emphasis on the restoration of the badly shaken Eastern alliances.

This displeased the British Government greatly and I happen to know that when the Blum Government fell on April 8th and the new Daladier Government was being formed, our Government did a great deal of wire pulling so that Paul Boncour should in no circumstances return to the Quai d'Orsay. Instead, it preferred a French Government with which it could co-operate on what one high authority called "A basis of give and take." There has been some give and take. The French have succeeded in persuading Chamberlain that Czechoslovakia cannot be abandoned to German aggression. Perhaps they persuaded him simply by convincing him beyond a doubt that if Czechoslovakia was invaded France would go to war, and England would have to come in sooner or later. On May 21st the British Government acted firmly because Czechoslovakia had mobilised and because France would have mobilised if Czechoslovakia had been attacked; and through the combination of these three displays of strength peace was saved. So much for the British "give"; but what about the British "take"? The "take" consists of two things—first, a rather weak French policy in relation to Spain; and secondly, France's consent to second England in the pressure that is being brought to bear on the Czech Government. No doubt nobody in France and England wants to fight for Czechoslovakia if a peaceful settlement of the Sudeten question can be reached—but one wonders whether the settlement that will be reached will not be fatal to Czechoslovakia's existence? It is significant that if until last month France was leading in the Anglo-French policy towards Czechoslovakia, this lead has been taken out of her hands by the Runciman mission. The "primary fact" had until then been France's determination to assist Czechoslovakia against aggression; the "primary fact" now is the Runciman report. What this Runciman report will be, I do not claim to know; and one can only hope that Lord Runciman will be careful not to recommend concessions which would, before long, open Czechoslovakia to the "peaceful aggression" of Germany. But, in any case, whatever he recommends, there is no certainty at all that Germany will accept his recommendations. In this sense, the situation will remain unchanged, and the Runciman mission cannot be regarded as being necessarily a contribution to peace in Europe. At its best it can only gain time. The dangerous aspect of the Runciman mission rests in the fact that it is being interpreted in Germany as an Anglo-French retreat from the strong position the two countries took up on May 21st.

vi. *Conclusion.*

A conclusion at the present stage is singularly difficult to make. Fearful errors have been made in the past; and many of those errors can no longer be repaired. The

League has been shattered; Austria has gone, and if no disaster has yet befallen France or England in Spain, it is largely because of the wonderful resistance of the Spanish Government in their fight against overwhelming odds. France and England should have two immediate objectives if they wish to avoid more serious trouble; they must not abandon Czechoslovakia for the mere pleasure of a brief respite—for that is all it can ever be if Germany gets a free hand in the East. Anglo-French firmness can alone reassure those League members who have lost faith in the League. Secondly, since it now seems too late to secure a complete victory of the Spanish Government, they must at least strive to attain a purely Spanish solution to the Spanish problem. A little rough handling of Italy in the Balearics would not be a bad beginning—now that it is again as clear as anything that Italy and Germany have no intention whatsoever of withdrawing their "volunteers." And it would not be a bad thing if the frontier to Spain were opened a little more widely. This would not be part of a "purely Spanish" solution, and would in fact be apt to prolong the war; but it would at least render an Italo-German solution of this war more remote. And the absence of an Italo-German victory in Spain is after all a considerable safeguard against a European war—for the strategic positions in Spain are indispensable to Italy if she desired to take part in such a war. Fortunately for us—though it is hard on the Spanish people—Franco and his allies are at present "otherwise engaged."

P.S.—In the course of this talk, delivered at Geneva on August 18, I almost—not quite, but almost—took it for granted that France would carry out her obligations to Czechoslovakia,—especially with her virtual certainty of British support. Alas, at the moment it looks as though the French were anxious, above all, not to save peace, but *to be left in peace at any price.* The Daladier Government is wobbling, and has asked Mr. Chamberlain to decide for them. If, after this, any Frenchman tells me that France could not help Czechoslovakia because "she wasn't sure of England," I shall laugh in his face. And I shall make my humble apologies to M. Flandin. But I still hope that France will not resign herself to becoming a second-class power. For, if she does, she may, before long, become a third-class power.

A.W.

Paris, September 18.

[History has added a further postscript—but the author's views as to all that the events of the past month may imply are clear throughout his paper.—Ed.]

CHAPTER VII

THE CAUSE AND CURE OF ARTICLE 16*

by

SENOR S. de MADARIAGA

Formerly Spanish Representative on the Council of the League of Nations

i. *Introduction.*

THIS somewhat enigmatical title was suggested to me by that of a book which some of you may have read: *Civilization, its Cause and Cure.* It is evident that according to whether we look at it in one way or another, civilisation may be considered as a blessing or as the reverse of a blessing. Similarly with Article 16, according to whether we look at it in one way or another, it may be considered as a blessing or it may be considered as an entirely different thing. I propose to examine the matter in a spirit of objectivity, at least in as objective a spirit as it is possible to muster in a world in which subjective considerations press themselves so tragically upon every one of us. There is a famous French quatrain:

> On est bête à Nanterre
> C'est la faute à Voltaire;
> Et sot à Palaiseau
> C'est la faute à Rousseau.

I do not propose, with your permission, to find fault with anyone, with man or nation, much as one might be

* Article XVI of the League of Nations Covenant.

tempted to do so. Were one to choose statesmen or states at which or at whom to throw stones, in connection with Article 16, the difficulty would be where to choose; for there is an ample choice of them. But stone-throwing is not constructive. I propose to consider the matter as objectively as I can, and, first, to define the problem as closely as possible.

ii. *Reasons for the Inclusion of Article* 16 *in the Covenant.*

I find that the problem is two-fold. First: why Article 16 at all? Then, why has it failed? For it does not seem evident why Article 16 should have been devised precisely when it turns up in world history, nor why, once written into our world charter it should have been so complete and disastrous a failure. This is my two-fold problem and, as happens with most problems of life, we can deal with it on different planes according to whether we delve more or less deeply into it.

Let me then begin by examining it on the first plane, that of purely legal and, up to a point, political relationships. It is evident that on this plane Article 16 is the inevitable outcome of the state of mind and of the state of politics that prevailed in Europe at the time when the treaties were drafted, the treaties of which the Covenant, as you know, is an integral part. If we have to understand why those treaties were drafted in such a way, obviously we have to look into the psychological roots of the treaties. And it is in them that we are going to discover the true causes of Article 16, at any rate on this first plane. First, the Peace Conference was obsessed by the impression of past dangers. Those who criticise the Peace Conference should nver forget that they are enjoying, or were enjoying until recently, a state of mental security which they owe, or owed, to those who drafted the treaty at the sacrifice of their own mental and physical security; for the people who drafted the treaty, however badly they drafted it, had just come through the agonies of a war of unheard-of destructive power, a war during which the western nations had undergone mortal danger when the vital line of defence, the link between France and Great Britain, had very nearly been broken through near Amiens and the Channel at the end of four years of war. So we have to remember, if our criticism is to be just, that the treaties were drafted by people who had passed through the tremendous agonies of the summer of 1918, and who were drafting this treaty which we all wanted to be a treaty of generosity and of permanent peace, about six months after they had passed through this terrific mental experience. Now this is a fact. This is no argument, this is neither defending, nor attacking, but just describing the position. But at the present moment there is in the world so much wildness, so much disregard for the objective conditions under which people live, whether they be right or wrong, as a result of these conditions, that it is, I believe, important now and then to reset our minds in an atmosphere of as much objectivity as we can.

That being so, it was obvious that the nations that drafted the treaty should be obsessed by the necessity of safeguarding themselves against that fear that they had experienced. For we must face the fact, they had been mortally afraid. It was then but natural that they should seek to incorporate into the treaty some means to ensure against the recurrence of similar dangers; and also that the method proposed and accepted should not have been the right one. But again, that is the inevitable outcome of the fact that the state of mind in which the problem was examined was not normal, but rather warped by the exceptional experience that the Allies had just undergone.

Next to this most important psychological root of Article 16 we must record a consciousness of guilt in the nations that drafted the treaty. Article 16 was not only the outcome of the fear of the past projected into the future, a kind of legal shield against dangers to come, but also the result of the feeling that, owing to the terms which they had made in other clauses of the treaty, that danger, which the near remembrance of the past led them to imagine as possible, would certainly recur, since unfortunately, led this time not by fear but by the other elementary feeling of man, greed, they had overstepped wisdom in the drafting of the treaty and they had grabbed even the enemy's territories, thereby destroying their claim that the war was a war for peace, for freedom and for the rights of peoples. If, in particular, the two leading nations, France and Great Britain, had not thought fit to take over the German colonies with reasons which to-day sound strangely false and hollow, that consciousness of guilt would not have come to strengthen the necessity for a shield against the danger of another war.

So far the causes. Now for the actual form of Article 16. There are technical and political reasons to explain it. The technical reason why the shield took the shape of Article 16 was that, possibly for the first time in history (though we should be sparing in the use of this formula, since events never happen in an entirely fresh form and therefore one can never say that a thing happens for the first time; it depends on what aspect of it we are concentrating our attention for the moment)—in certain aspects, then, for the first time in history nations had found that war could be fought on such an immense scale that it was impossible for any one nation or for any one man to master it. When we go back to our own memories of those days, nothing impresses the mind more deeply than the utter disproportion between the size of the men and the size of the events with which they had to deal. When we think of those really eminent men called Foch, Jellicoe, Ludendorf, and we think of the events they had to handle, we find they were like corks in the water imagining that they commanded the waves when it was actually the waves that tossed them. The movements of troops, the problems of food, the problems of information, etc., had outgrown the capacity of the human mind. The strategic situation of the two central powers made them so dangerous that the nations of the west had to organise an alliance of practically the whole world except Germany and Austro-Hungary in order to reduce them to peace and even then not without having gone through that tremendous danger of 1918. This technical reason, the fact that war had become universal and totalitarian, led the Peace Conference to imagine a system of guarding against the coming war by means of a universal insurance against it. It was in reality the writing down of all that had been done during the war in a different form and in a pre-established way. The nations had united against a common danger; they had been led to setting up special organisations for pooling their resources. By reversing this empirical process, Article 16 was, so to speak, pre-figured without anybody having to spend too much brain power on the matter. It was all there. Life gave the solution during the war. It was then put into the Covenant and called Article 16 because as happens with all of us, nations or individuals, whenever we have gone through an experience we codify and file it for the next event.

Politically, the system had to be made a little more complicated, for, evidently, we could not call on anybody to ensure anybody without conditions; and it became necessary to organise a general system, a kind of legal basis for the structure of Article 16. At this time, we begin to notice a kind of dual tendency inside the system. The pacifist says: wars are due to armaments, so let us disarm first and then there will be no war; the politician says: armaments are due to wars, therefore let us first abolish war, then we will disarm. Now, if we read the Covenant with attention, we will find that these two ways of thinking were present in the minds of the drafters, and first the one, then the other, held the field. Thus in Article 8 when it is said that nations must disarm—it was at any rate *meant*, by the pacifist. But the politician toned it down to "must reduce their armaments to the lowest point consistent with national safety and with international obligations." Then the pacifist came back on that and added that those obligations must be only those enforced by common action. You can see in a sentence like that three or four successive interventions coming now from the pacifist, now from the politician, in order to keep the balance of the system.

So much for the system which it is hardly necessary to define here in more detail. The upshot of it all is that, as a result of these psychological and technical reasons, the Covenant set down an insurance against war which is known as the system of collective security. This is a rather rapid, and therefore rather inexact phrase. What is meant is not a system of collective security at all, but a system of collective insurance of the security of every single nation which is an entirely different proposition. In fact, if I may anticipate my conclusion now, the system of collective security has failed because it is not really a system of collective security, but only let me say again, a system of collective insurance of individual (national) security. I will come to a more detailed demonstration of this point as I develop the several planes in which I propose to examine the matter.

iii. *Why Has Collective Security Been a Failure?* (a) *In Theory.*

Of the two-fold problem that we are examining, first that Article 16 is there and second that Article 16 has failed, I have on this first plane of legal relations given my reasons why Article 16 is there; still on this plane, let me now try to give my reasons for its failure. It has failed for a double set of reasons. First for what we might call theoretical reasons and then for reasons of practice. From the theoretical angle it has failed for a number of causes. The first because the relationship between Articles 8 and 16 has not been given adequate weight. After all, Article 8 is the first Article in the system of collective security. It is even the first Article in the Covenant because the first seven articles are only articles on League structure, not on League working. Up to Article 7 we are told that an association is formed, who is going to govern, how the secretariat is to be organised, and so forth. And the first article in which a League task is described, i.e. what the association is for, is Article 8. Surely this shows that the pacifist school had the upper hand there and that they decided that, whatever happened, as soon as League Members had done with the details of organisation and secretariat, and so forth, they would begin with disarmament. That was but natural, for a system of collective security was being planned, that is a system of collective insurance, and therefore disarmament was a first prerequisite, for if Article 8 were realised, if disarmement were achieved, the application of Article 16 would be enormously simplified. There are two reasons for this. First because, if nations are disarmed they will find it far more difficult to attack anyone and, second, because even if they do attack it will be easier to reduce them to obedience. One might have thought that since Article 8 and Article 16 had been accepted by all the members of the League, there would have been no difficulty in reducing armaments there and then on the basis of the Covenant. But we have been witnessing for years the effort of some nations to increase the credit side of collective security before they were willing to grant anything on the debit side of disarmament. That is one of the most important reasons for the failure of Article 16.

The second clause of the failure of Article 16 was the weakness of Article 19. Obviously a system which aims at organising collective security must provide for the movement of life. Life cannot be static. We have decided that at one particular moment the world is going to have a certain figure, but life must go on. The shape of things will change and it is not going to remain faithful to the shape we decided in our treaty; so we must provide for growth. Article 19 has provision for growth, but is notoriously insufficient in itself and I need not waste any time in proving the point. I just note the fact.

There are other legal insufficiencies in the system which have had a considerable moral effect in weakening its authority; in particular the several loopholes that national sovereignty has reserved for itself in the application of Article 15, the study of which would repay the time devoted to it. I should also mention under this heading the astonishing way in which the provisions of Articles 18 and 20 have been neglected in Geneva. To begin with they were separated in drafting and that was a great mistake because, in my opinion, the Covenant would have been much clearer if Articles 18 and 20 had been drafted together in one article. Article 18 must be explained in relation to Article 20. Article 18 says that treaties, in order to be valid, must be registered in Geneva. Article 20 stipulates that no Member-State must enter into or retain any diplomatic or legal obligations incompatible with the Covenant. It is obvious that if you put together these two articles, all treaties, on being registered in Geneva, should be not merely registered as you register a trunk in a station, but examined to see whether they are compatible with the Covenant according to Article 20. The Council ought to have been in a position to say, in every case, whether or not it would accept registration according to whether the treaty was or was not compatible with the Covenant. Had such a system been organised, a certain number of things would not have occurred. Things happen which might not have happened if organisation had been different, because the eventual effect of the organisation on them would have been discounted beforehand. For instance, if the League had seen fit to apply Article 18 in the sense just outlined, that extraordinary exchange of letters between the British Government and the Italian Government over Abyssinia in 1925 would not have occurred because the British Government, being perhaps somewhat more squeamish than the Italian, would have preferred not to be told by the Council: "We are very sorry, but these letters cannot be registered since they are not compatible with Article 20 of the Covenant."

Further still on the legal aspects of the system, the main cause of the weakness of collective security has no doubt been that the United States did not ratify it. It is obvious that the system had been thought out with America in. With America out, the system became an entirely different proposition and it is absolutely useless and frivolous, and it has been useless and frivolous for twenty years, to be told that America is willing and will do everything she can do to help the League; for it is obvious, if you look at the system, that nothing short of full membership from the outset of the conflict can serve any useful purpose. There is time for politeness and there is time for sparing feelings; but there is time for truth; 90 per cent of the trouble of the world is due to the fact that the United States did not join the League of Nations—with every possible respect to the United States—but facts are facts. I am not accusing anyone and I am far too unimportant to apportion merit or guilt. But I am explaining, and on the plane of explanation the fact that the League motor-car lacked its main cylinder is obviously important in order to show why it has not run.

iii. *Why Has Collective Security Been a Failure?* (b) *In Practice.*

So much for theoretical considerations. Now practice. Covering the whole practice of the system, the main reason why Article 16 and the system in general has failed is that business of this kind is always brought to the League far too late. When was the Abyssinian question brought to the League? When there was but little hope for us to stay Italy on the path to war. When was the Manchurian question brought to the League? When there was no hope of staying Japan on the path of spoliation. It is evident that *the system of collective security implies a system of collective policy.* For, as at present understood, the system comes to this: Nations do what they like; when all goes well, they kill the beast and keep the skin; if all does not go well, they run to Geneva for help from the others. Is this fair? Has it any sense or has it too much sense? Would to God—or to whomever He delegates world affairs—that this criticism were merely theoretical. It is all too practical. If you take either the Manchurian or the Abyssinian case you will find to what a tremendous extent the colonial past of some great nations has prevented the League from putting the brake on to other big nations; in other words, the "good" nations are not good enough to keep the "bad" nations in order and the remembrance of the colonial history of the colonial nations has been one of the most important amongst the factors which prevented an effective use of the Covenant in the Manchurian and in the Abyssinian cases. Again, I am accusing no one. Of course not. Human faults have been there for a long time; they will be there for a long time to come. I am only explaining that, since the League of Nations was an effort of the human beast to rise a little above beasthood, it was obvious that the human beast would find it very difficult to keep on its hind legs and would fall back on its front legs again; and the result is that, when we tried to put sense and decency and legal effort and legal order into the colonial expansion of European nations, all the colonial past rose up against us and those that should have helped us most found themselves prevented from doing so because they still remembered their own recent adventures.

Let us recall two facts. About Manchuria: several years ago, in 1927, England chose to forget all about the Covenant and sent a fleet to Shanghai. About Abyssinia. In 1925, by an exchange of letters which I have already mentioned, England, a member of the League, and Italy, also a member of the League, decided to divide between themselves Abyssinia, which was a third member of the League, without even troubling to tell her anything about it. "Zones of influence," if you like, but still we all know what that means.

Another point, most important in practice, is that of the relations between Articles 11 and 16. Evidently, Article 11 is the main article of the Covenant. Article II is the Covenant. And so far as I am concerned, if I could get the promise of all the nations that Article II would be applied in full, I could let all the other articles go. All the Covenant is there. But that is why some nations, helped by some people who ought to have known better, have always prevented us from applying it. Let me remind you that both in the Manchurian and in the Abyssinian cases the two nations that had taken the—

let us call it—lively part in the incidents, insisted on keeping the Council at bay by arguing that the matter should be transacted under direct negotiations. *Direct negotiations are a direct lie to Article* 11. Article 11 means there must be *no direct negotiation.* That is what it means; and yet we had to wait on direct negotiations because we were told " if you let us arrange that, we will find a way out." It is, of course, a very well-known fact that the burglar does not like the arrival of the police or even of friendly neighbours.

When the Council met in April, 1935, immediately after the Stresa Conference, and we called the attention of the Italian Government to the movement of troops being sent to Eritrea and Somaliland, we were told that Eritrea and Somaliland were Italian territory and the Council had nothing to do with it. Now that is a totally unwarranted conclusion. There is nothing in Article 11 to mean that the " circumstance " which is dangerous enough for the League to take cognisance of and act accordingly, must not be one within the " sovereignty " of a nation. There is nothing of the kind in Article 11. In Article 11 it is said that the League has the right and the duty to take a hand in any circumstance likely to disturb the peace of the world. It is obvious that if to-day, *inside Germany,* Hitler decided to mobilise in such a way as to justify the fear that he was preparing an attack on a particular nation, it would be the right and the duty of the Council to take a hand in the matter, even though the movements of troops would take place entirely within the sovereignty of the nation concerned.*

* In law. I am not referring to what would be politics, wise or useful in the present instance with a maimed League.

Finally there was again the rule of unanimity. It all comes to this: is commonsense a rule of law or is it not? If commonsense is a rule of law it must override the article of the Covenant in which it is said that unless the contrary be expressly stated, the Covenant must be applied by unanimity; but, if in applying the Covenant by unanimity, the article which is applied does not make sense, obviously unanimity must go by the board. If we apply Article 10 by unanimity it has no sense. Belgium invades Holland. You apply Article 10. Under Article 4 Belgium becomes a member of the Council for this affair. The question is put: has Article 10 been violated? And Belgium says no. As you have bound yourselves to apply the rule of unanimity, there is nothing more to do. This does not make sense, and therefore the rule of unanimity must wait upon the rule of sense; but this is a point on which the legal experts of the big powers are obdurate. For them, sense is a rule of law only if it suits the interests of the particular nation.

This is my first plane. I have now given the reasons why on the plane of legal and political relations Article 16 exists and the reasons why it has failed. But there are several other planes on which the same two points may be taken up again. First, Article 16 is the outcome of a wrong parallel between men and nations. A few men enter into an association of "collective security" or rather of collective insurance of individual security. They can do it, for they can move about, they can take a train, they can arm themselves, hire a car, ride a horse, gather, and disperse. Men have the privilege of mobility, like animals. Nations have no such privilege. Nations have the immobility of vegetables, of trees. It may be argued that they can send armies and navies and air fleets considerable distances. The fact that the British fleet can travel about the world adds but little, it expands but little the vegetable immobility of Great Britain. It means that Great Britain has a certain number of offshoots, all limited, for armies, navies and air fleets need BASES. The nation cannot move. You cannot use it and send it off where you want it to be. The immobility of nations is absolute and therefore it is absurd to imagine that we are going to move them about for the defence of any one of them against another.

However, whether fought as a result of Article 16 or fought against Article 16, *War is a thing in itself.* War is a phenomenon of nature, since human society is a part of nature and war is an event of human society. War is a phenomenon of the world of nations. I am not saying that *therefore* war must remain for ever a part of nations. I am one of those who believe that war is going to disappear from the world, and quite soon. Cannibalism is part of nature and has practically disappeared. War is cannibalism and it is going to disappear, but not by Article 16, because Article 16 is a system whereby a few nations say: if one nation tries to eat another nation, all the other nations will eat the first. Why won't this work? Because war as a social phenomenon has its own natural laws. I am not referring to those well-meaning but feeble laws of war drafted every now and then by good souls to teach table manners to the tiger. I am referring to the laws of war as a phenomenon of the society of nations. As soon as war is on the horizon, as soon as war is in our minds as a hypothesis, the *pattern* changes. As soon as the atmosphere changes from peace to war the tensions that link together all these trees called nations change entirely, and the pattern becomes quite different. Let us consider a nation like Switzerland. In the pattern of peace, I daresay the most important nations for Switzerland are the United States and England, where tourists come from. If the pattern changes to one of war, the three nations that matter most for Switzerland are Germany, France and Italy. Let us take another case, Spain for instance. In time of peace, the nations that matter for Spain are France, England and the United States, where trade comes from. In time of war, if the war is going to implicate the South American nations—because there again the pattern of war will depend on the kind of war—the nations that matter for Spain are the nations that speak her language and live her civilisation. Spain will never be able to apply sanctions to the South American nations, nor Great Britain to the United States or to her own Dominions.

Article 16, thoroughly applied means war. Once at war, no matter the cause, we are at war under the spirit of war. Nothing can explain that better than a glance at what happens when the individual soul passes from peace to war. Suppose that England has to fight a war, whether it is a war of Article 16 or whether it is a war to get another colony in the teeth of Article 16. The war will be fought remembering the Union Jack and remembering Grenville and Drake and Nelson, and the blue jackets, and the red coats and the glory of England. And it cannot be otherwise. War is not fought with mere armaments but with the war-spirit drawn from the animal instincts of man and from the "glories" of history. Now ninety-nine per cent of that is alien to the Covenant.

Article 16 therefore necessitates the maintenance of that which it sets out to punish and to destroy. In a room here in Geneva, the present Italian Ambassador in London, who was then Foreign Secretary of Mussolini, had once a tremendous success in showing to the world to what extent Italy was a devoted servant of collective security, of peace and of the League of Nations. But simultaneously, Mussolini was issuing a most bellicose catechism to train Italians from the very earliest age to use a gun, to raise and sharpen the war-spirit of Italy. What could France and England do? Were they going to say to Mussolini "Stop that war-like education"? Mussolini would have answered: "Stop the red coats; stop the blue jackets, haul down the Union Jacks; do not speak any more about Napoleon to children in the schools; scratch off from the Arc de Triomphe the names of his battles all over Europe." How can we solve that problem, how can we, so long as we remain attached to a system of war for curing war, prevent war by making war? We cannot. War may be fought under the flag of the League of Nations, or under the Union Jack. But in either case, war consists in taking the human being back several centuries to make him able to kill other men. I am describing the facts of nature. It is evident that as long as Article 16 is there with war at the end of it, war cannot be driven off the face of the Earth.

On a more general plane. Why is Article 16 there? Why has it failed? It is there because inventions and the human intellect have woven the communities of the world into one community only. We have discovered so many ways of improving communications that the world is one market, however disorganised, one public opinion however divided against itself; and therefore, because of this solidarity amongst us, we have written an article of the Covenant to translate this solidarity in the scheme of things into a solidarity for insuring against war. Having pooled our business and our interests, we aimed also at pooling our way of making war and of guarding against it. Only one thing lags behind and that is our own acknowledgment of the unity of this market and of the unity of this world state. The world is like a huge monster with only one body and fifty heads (mostly with but poor brains inside) as a result of which we are in this uncomfortable phase of history: if we were not one body it would not matter that we have fifty heads. If we had one head it would not matter that we have but one body. Having one body and fifty heads, such is the cause of the failure of Article 16. Article 16 is there because the solidarity of mankind is a fact. Article 16 has failed because the solidarity of mankind is not recognised as such by men. Until we have only one head and only one heart, until we have unified our ambitions and our feelings and once made one conscious community, we cannot apply sanctions because the fifty heads will be at loggerheads.

iv. *Conclusion.*

And now yet another plane. Article 16 was born of fear and fear is negative and Article 16 therefore uses the language of negativeness. The Covenant of the League of Nations, in its Preamble defines the aims of the League: "to promote international co-operation and to achieve international peace and security." But who ever decides to "unite and co-operate"? Anyone invited to do so would ask, " May I know what you want me to co-operate in and what for? " There is nothing positive in this document but only negative repression: of illicit traffic in opium, of the traffic in women and children, of armaments, of aggression. The Covenant is the result of repressed souls, the result of souls that spent four years of their life under the shadow of war and therefore under a dreadful repression. To be sure, the Covenant adds " To achieve international peace and security." But does anyone who is normal and healthy want peace and security? Can you imagine a young man of twenty meeting a pretty girl and saying " Let us have peace and security "? He will know very well that his proposal will bring many things, good and bad to both, but not peace, and not security. When a human being is healthy he wants to create things, he wants to do things, he wants to risk things, but he wants neither peace nor security, though they will come by the way. This Preamble is due to the disastrous strain on the human soul as a result of that inhuman war of 1914-18. This Preamble must go and instead of it something positive and creative must be put forward, from which the peace of the world will result precisely when it is not sought as such. All the work of the world is waiting: merchant marine, world traffic, aviation, seeing to it that human races are not downtrodden and persecuted. More life, more positiveness, more common and intelligent purpose and never mention peace, never mention war. Then when you neither mention peace nor war, then may we expect war to disappear and peace to reign amongst men.

And finally, the last plane of all. Let us read the beginning of Article 16:

> " Should any member of the League resort to war in disregard of its Covenants under Articles 12, 13 or 15, it shall *ipso facto* be deemed to have committed an act of war against all other members of the League . . . . "

It shall be deemed. By whom? The English jurists who drafted this sentence, drafted it in the innocence of their minds, using the English formula, for in England " it shall be deemed " has an obvious legal sense : it means : well, if you ask an English lawyer " What do you mean by ' it shall be deemed? ' " he will open his eyes like saucers, if he has an eye-glass his eye-glass will fall. He will say, " I don't know, I suppose it means, ' it shall be deemed.' " Why? Because for the English jurist the existence of England is such an obvious thing that he is not aware of it, just as we are not aware of the air we breathe. He writes " it shall be deemed " without realising that this document is not going to apply to the English community, but to a vaster community of which English is but a part.

The English community is one of the strongest communities in the world. Owing to that magnificent gift of the British race which makes of any Englishman the whole of England, that " it shall be deemed " means " by England." But the Covenant is to apply to the world, and the jurist does not realise that.

Who is the world? No one is the world. Those who know Geneva know very well that in the Council and the Assembly the world is nowhere. The Estonian is thinking of Estonia, the Lithuanian is thinking of Lithuania, the New Zealander of New Zealand, and so on, but no one is thinking of the world. Yet Article 16 was drafted because these English jurists were under the impression that the world existed as a conscious community living, like England, in men's hearts. But the world does not exist yet that way and therefore, until the world exists as a community, that is to say until there is in us the living sense that we are the world, Article 16 cannot work. But on the other hand, when a number of us, a sufficient number of us, are convinced that the world exists as a community, Article 16 will no longer be necessary.

CHAPTER VIII

HOW CAN THE AGGREGSSOR BE STOPPED?

by

ANDREW ROTHSTEIN

Geneva Correspondent for Tass (Soviet News Agency)

THE main question facing all of us to-day is, how are we to stop the aggressors? I say " all of us " advisedly. Tens of millions of people like ourselves are to-day living under the shells, air bombs, rapine and massacre of the aggressor forces. Millions of others are living in the shadow of these horrible things. More than that: thousands of young Englishmen and Americans have felt impelled to leave their homes and their jobs during the last two years, in order to go with their comrades from other countries and strike a blow at the aggressors—in many cases to give their lives—precisely because they felt that aggression was having too much of its own way in the world. Many of you no doubt know—or knew—some of these young men. All of us here to-day, young or old, men and women, may quite reasonably expect ourselves to be called upon at any moment to follow where they led, whether we like it or no, if their sacrifice proves to be insufficient to stop the tide of aggression.

i. *The Forces Which Made and Changed the League.*

I would rather put the problem in its most general form—how to stop the aggressors—than in the narrower form proposed to me of " commitments to coerce," because that title might create the impression that legal obligations are the primary thing when we are seeking to preserve peace: and that way lies illusion, confusion and disillusionment, which have helped the aggressors quite enough already. Legal obligations are very important, but even more important, for those who are seeking to make them effective, is the movement of the forces which brought those obligations into being. The greatest and most far-reaching legal obligation ever undertaken in human history was that multilateral international treaty known as the Covenant of the League of Nations; but all of you know the disillusionment and despair which have spread because that legal obligation, with all its moral force, has not proved sufficient to protect China, Abyssinia, Spain or Austria.

Yet a sober consideration of the forces which brought the League into existence, and of the changes which they have undergone since, will not only show the futility of such despair, but will teach us how to turn into decisive victories those reverses which world peace and law have suffered at the hands of the aggressor Powers.

Why did the League come into existence? In 1919 the world was still sickened and distracted with the hideous slaughter and ruin of the most terrible war in history. Millions of men in all countries were armed, they knew the strength of their arms, they had seen great Empires and, in one country, the capitalist system itself, overturned by the force of those arms. Above all those men, and the millions of working men and women whom the war had taught the utter dependence of the modern State on the good will of the working class, were demanding an assurance of security and peace. So were the dozens of smaller

States who had played a secondary part in the war, or had been its victims, or had come into existence in consequence of it. The alliance of Great Powers which had won the war required a form of legal sanction for their conquests, and for the other territorial and economic arrangements which they subsequently devised in the Peace Treaties. Within each country, the ruling classes found different means of answering—and deceiving—the demand of the people for economic and political security at home; on the international field, their reply was the compromise embodied in the Covenant of the League of Nations.

When I say compromise, I have in mind the extreme looseness and vagueness of its drafting. The Great Powers who were responsible for the Covenant were too conscious of their own Empires, and of their methods of protecting them from within and without, to be over-exact in drafting obligations about minorities, or disarmament, or the repression of aggression.

Nevertheless the Covenant did enshrine one important practical lesson which the peoples had drawn from the experience of the last war; that they could reap only untold misery from the forcible redrawing of international frontiers, and that whoever attempted to do so, whatever his excuse, was an enemy of the human race, against whom the whole of humanity ought to unite. The knowledge that the ruling classes of the defeated Powers had, in their moment of triumph over disarmed Russia in 1918, imposed a Peace Treaty at least as bad as Versailles, made it easier to come to these conclusions. They helped to make the Covenant, with all its imperfections, a potential barrier to war.

What has happened during these 19 years to the forces

that brought the League into being? The existing economic and social system has made immense advances, not only in industrial technique, but also in the acuteness of its internal contradictions and of its crises. The mass of the people in every country, if they retain but dim memories of the way they were swindled after the war, have had in return the lessons of the frightful world economic crisis of 1930-33, and undoubtedly are more politically active—particularly in their hatred of war—than in the years before 1914. Their struggle is now vastly reinforced by the existence, in place of Tsarist Russia, of a Socialist Great Power which, because of its very nature, carries on a constant fight for peace. The smaller States are just as vitally interested in the preservation of peace as they were in 1919. They are far more alarmed about its prospects than they were then, because the German Empire, revived in its most aggressive and terrorist form—that of Fascism—has gone far in its preparations for a new general redivision of the world (Goebbels has told us so) by war. Japan and Italy gained least from the last war, but their imperialist appetites are only enhanced by that fact, and by the Fascist nature of their internal regimes; and they have joined forces with Germany. The great Empires which won the last war are just as concerned as they were in 1919 to hold on to the spoils, and are arming feverishly to do so: for they do not believe in a peaceful redistribution of the world for purposes of exploitation, any more than Goebbels. But so far, for reasons which I propose to deal with a little later, they have declined to call upon the mass of the people in their own countries to join forces with the U.S.S.R. and the vast majority of other States interested in keeping the peace, in order to repel the aggressor as the League Covenant provides.

In fairness I ought to add that this failure to apply the Covenant did not begin when Japan and Germany came on the scene, but many years before—in fact, at the very foundation of the League, when the Powers who drafted its Covenant, and were its first signatories, were waging a war of aggression (not known in those days as "non-intervention") upon Soviet Russia. Turkey, Greece and China are other States which experienced this inconsistency in the early years of the League, at the hands of its founders.

At all events, the radical shift in the correlation of international forces which has taken place since 1919 should be sufficient to explain why a Covenant which in reality, at the moment of its signature, was the expression of the *particular* balance of power, social as well as political, at a *given* moment, is not now being put into effect by its authors. Some of their spokesmen, indeed, as Lord Halifax's memorable speech on Ethiopia at the last League Council showed, are rather inclined to regard it as a somewhat irritating "scrap of paper"—or, if you prefer a more homely metaphor, as some old and extravagant love-letter, produced at an awkward moment in a breach-of-promise suit. I mean the speech in which Lord Halifax contrasted "the ideal of devotion, unflinching but unpractical, to some high purpose" with "the ideal of a practical victory for peace" in order to justify possible recognition of the Italian conquest.

But I must insist again, as I did at the beginning, that, important as violations of the Covenant and other treaties by some, and their non-observance by others, undoubtedly are, the material fact which lies behind these legal facts far transcends them in importance. That material fact is that, reckoning only the populations of Ethiopia, of Spain and its colonies, of China and of Japan and its colonies, over 580 million people—or more than one-quarter of the population of the world—are already directly involved in war on a large scale, and for the most part are suffering all its horrors. You will notice that I have not included in this total the people of Germany and Italy, although many of the privations of war have already come their way. In face of this tremendous fact, and of the sinister hint of still wider conflict conveyed by such events as the fighting on the Soviet-Manchurian frontier and the German intimidation of Czechoslovakia, talk of "the danger of war" as of some remote possibility, and attempts to treat its problems as those of the international lawyer or the professional mediator, are deceptive and dangerous. Peace or war to-day is an issue that the peoples have to decide, around the definite issue of how to arrest the aggressions begun and planned by the Triple Alliance of aggressors—Germany, Japan and Italy.

ii. *How Not to Stop the Aggressor.*

Various methods of stopping the aggressors have been attempted in recent years. One is to do nothing about it, or even to help the aggressor, in the hope that he will be satisfied with one victim. Experience, however, shows that this hope is illusory. Thus, directly Italian aggression began, Ethiopia was subjected to an arms embargo—formally applied to both sides, of course—and to the closing of the French railway to arms traffic; while later, at the critical moment of the war, Great Britain and France refused to consider stopping oil deliveries to Italy, although they were assured of Soviet support. This did not prevent, it only encouraged, Mussolini's subsequent attack on the Spanish Republic. During the Italo-German war on Spain, in its turn, destruction of British, French and other lives and property has been borne without retaliation, and on the contrary the invaders have been helped by a blockade of Republican Spain, organised by the British and French Governments, and by the withholding of the gold which is its property, and with which the Spanish Government designed to buy food for its starving women and children. None of these efforts have availed to win the friendship of Mussolini, or kind words from his press—let alone any diminution of Italian activities in Palestine, Egypt or Tunis. In 1931-32 Japan was allowed to take Manchuria from China, and in 1937-38 to wage a first-class war on China, with only paper protests and offers of mediation in the first instance, and then, as time went on, with direct British assistance to Japan, in the shape of an agreement to share in the spoils of Japan's robbery of the Chinese Customs, and quite lately of a refusal to grant financial assistance to China, when she badly needs it to buy war material. Can anyone say that Japan's attitude to the League Powers was any friendlier, after twelve months of such tactics, than at the outset? Or take the case of Germany. In 1935 Hitler was able to secure the Naval Treaty with Great Britain, in defiance of a League resolution condemning the unilateral violation of treaties; and in 1936 he was allowed without resistance to remilitarise the Rhineland. These tolerated revisions of the Versailles Treaty encouraged him to prepare and carry out, in 1938, the military occupation and annexation of Austria—with no more comment from the French and British Governments than a flat refusal by the British Prime Minister, in the House of Commons two days before the occupation, to warn him against such action. And what was it, on the night of May 20-21 of this year, that stopped the German armies from marching into Czechoslovakia: grateful recognition of kindnesses rendered by the British and French Governments, or the knowledge that the Czechoslovak Army, fully prepared, and backed by the French General Staff and the Red Army, was waiting for them?

Another method that has been tried is that of an appeal to the better nature of the aggressors. I am not aware whether in the United States there is anyone with the unique position of Mr. George Lansbury, but I am sure that you have no one there half as active in this direction. What result could one hope for, from the application of this method? If you are seriously exercised about the reply, read that terrible book brought out by Gollancz, *What War Means,* by Mr. H. J. Timperley, the *Manchester Guardian* correspondent in China; or read the young Mussolini's account of his exploits in Ethiopia; or the extracts from Hitler's views on policy in general and frightfulness in particular, extracted from *Mein Kampf* and contained in the useful threepenny pamphlets published by the "Friends of Europe." You will find many eminent examples of theory coinciding with practice in the field of ruthlessness, but very little evidence to show that it would not be a more promising task to train a man-eating tiger into a household pet.

A third method that has been advocated has been to

appeal to the aggressors' commercial instincts, and to satisfy their fancied wants by writing off their debts, giving them a big loan as the price of abandoning " autarky," and handing over to them for exploitation colonial or other territories, rich in raw material and cheap labour. I do not propose to discuss now whether it is tolerable that peoples should be bought and sold in this way, merely because in the past they have been conquered : or whether it is at all likely that any Empire will voluntarily hand over any of its colonies, even in the very transparent guise of transference to a " League mandate." I would like you to consider it solely from the angle from which it has been considered more than once, here in Geneva—that of expediency. Let me add, in parenthesis, that we have a few advocates of such a solution at Geneva, all ardent champions of its chief spokesman in Europe, M. Van Zeeland. And from the angle of expediency, the fly in the ointment is that no one has yet been able to suggest any means by which the world could be guaranteed that such aid would not be transformed into a simple method of financing aggression. M. Van Zeeland certainly does not suggest any such guarantee in his famous plan. On the contrary, he looks the problem boldly in the face—saying that he " understands such preoccupation " and that political guarantees " ought to be given-"—and passes on, to make the exactly opposite suggestion; that Germany and Italy, with Britain, France and the U.S.A., should reorganise world economic relations first, and that *then* might begin the search for " the political conditions of a durable peace." By that time Marshal Goering would certainly not require his four-year plan for turning butter into guns, since credits, loans and raw materials from abroad would supply him with all the guns *and* butter that he required.

This flaw in the schemes for financing the aggressor States has been pointed out again and again in the various economic and financial committees of the League. It was the cause of last year's Assembly laying down that international co-operation, both in the economic and the political fields, " must be based on the renunciation of recourse to violence and war as instruments of policy, and on the strict observance of international obligations." Let me mention, in passing, that this resolution was, most appropriately, put forward on the joint initiative of the Brtiish, French and Soviet delegations. It brings us back, however, to our point of departure : how are the aggressor States to be induced to renounce violence and treaty-breaking?

Another method that perforce has been applied during all these years is to pass more or less condemnatory resolutions at League meeting; in other words, to try and mobilise public opinion against the aggressors. I am very far from decrying that method, but you will probably agree with me that it has proved very inadequate as a means of stopping aggression. Moreover, recent practice seems to indicate that, in the absence of some effective means of following them up, even such resolutions are becoming more and more unpopular and improbable. At the last Assembly, the resolution on Spain was rejected because it mentioned the well-known fact that there are " veritable foreign army corps " in Spain. On China, the British and French delegations successfully opposed the use of the word " aggression "—involving the pains and penalties of the Covenant—in describing the Japanese invasion of China. To-day we have the spectacle of Poland announcing that it will not seek re-election to the League Council, obviously—as the attitude of the Polish representative on the Council during the last twelve months clearly shows—in order to avoid the unpleasant necessity of saying where it stands, when the Council discusses future cases of flagrant aggression.

iii. *The Peace Bloc: Pros and Cons.*

We come back, then, to the principal question: "How are we to stop the aggressor? "I think it must be perfectly plain that there is only one way to stop him, and that is to talk to him in language that he can understand; in other words, to bring together into one bloc all the potential victims of aggression and the Powers interested in the preservation of peace, and to threaten the aggressor States with the use of overwhelming force, unless they desist from their present aggressions, and abandon their plans in that direction for the future. That, be it noted, would restore the position which the Covenant itself has in mind, in its fifteenth and sixteenth articles, and which Edgar Mowrer, as you will remember, put in a nutshell, when he said that "readiness to stop aggression anywhere by force is the kernel of the League." In the case of present aggression, such a threat would clearly have to be the corollary of definite action in favour of the victim—such, for example, as the granting of a large loan to China, and the imposition of an embargo on Japan; or the opening of the French frontier and the armaments markets to the Spanish Republic, and the giving of notice to quit to the Italian and German troops in Spain (in the first instance, to the nest of air bandits in Majorca).

How Can the Aggressor be Stopped?

One question that arises immediately is: "Can the aggressor be stopped by the threat of force?" The answer is, yes. It has been done. In January, 1937, the threat of France and Great Britain to use force brought to a standstill, at least temporarily, overhasty German attempts to "dig in" in Morocco. In September, 1937, a similar threat, this time in combination with a group of Powers interested in the Mediterranean trade, put a definite stop to the piratical activities of Italian "unknown submarines." I have already mentioned the case of May 21 in Czechoslovakia; it is no fault of the method if Great Britain has given new heart to German aggression by continuing her pressure on the Czechoslovak Republic, instead of trying, for a change, a little pressure on the Nazi aggressors. This month there has been the Changkoufeng case in the Far East, in which it was not only the actual Soviet force with which they were faced that drove back the Japanese military, but the knowledge that they were drawing down upon themselves the whole force of the U.S.S.R., in circumstances which made discretion the better part of valour for their allies in Europe. All these cases have shown that even a partial and *extempore* display of force can throw back the aggressor.

Another question that is often asked is: "Would not this mean general war?" The answer is that, on the contrary, it is the opposite tactics that are slowly but inevitably, as both experience and common sense tell us, leading the world to general war. It is hesitation and pusillanimity which incite the Fascist bully, not the display of a bold front. Take but one example, out of the many I could quote. You may be aware that there is but one Power which, from October, 1936, onwards, has consistently given material aid to the Spanish Republic (I am not speaking, of course, of voluntary collections, which began among its citizens directly the rebellion started). It so happens that the States attacking Spain—Germany and Italy—regard themselves as peculiarly ordained by Providence to destroy that particular Power. The Power I have in mind was labouring under extraordinary difficulties in rendering this assistance, not only because of geography, but still more because of politics, in that it had incurred the high displeasure of the British and French Governments for its aid to the Spanish Republic. There was no serious ground for belief, at least until this year, that the British and French Governments would have lifted a finger if the Fascist " axis " had decided to attack that Power. Yet so enormous were the difficulties with which the aggressor States would have been confronted, in the event of such an attack—difficulties not only of a military nature, but of an economic and social nature in their own countries—that they did not venture to attack that *single* Power. What becomes, then, of the argument repeatedly advanced, in the course of the war in Spain, as the excuse for one piece of poltroonery after another, that " if Great Britain and France also helped the Spanish Republic, it might let loose a general war "?

Let me point out in passing that, just as bullying is infectious, so is its collapse. A blow to any section of the " axis " must obviously react on the other sections, which are only strong while they are together. I am very interested in what Edgar Mowrer has said, as to the opinion of foreign observers in China on the probable effect in European affairs of the weakening of Japan; namely, to induce greater moderation in the rulers of

Germany. It so happens that a very responsible person in Czechoslovakia said to me, a very few weeks ago, how deeply the gallant stand of the Chinese people was appreciated in his country, for absolutely practical reasons which I will leave you to think out for yourselves.

The previous question supplies the answer to a third conundrum which the Fascists themselves are fond of posing, because it is part of the bluff on which they rely; namely, that they are irresistible, if it comes to an actual trial of strength. One aspect of this question is that of what is called "war potential." A good many calculations of this have been made in recent months. The latest that occurs to me can be found in the book by Elwyn Jones, *The Battle for Peace.* Briefly, it points out that the resources of the Fascist axis in coal and oil, in metals and raw materials, in manpower and foodstuffs, are so much smaller than those of their presumable opponents—the British and French Empires, the U.S.S.R., Czechoslovakia and other smaller European countries, with the U.S.A. in the background—that in a general war they would not be able to stay the course. More particularly—and this is the other aspect—because Germany has had to introduce ration cards and substitutes in relatively peacetime conditions, just as Italy has had to do with war bread; while one year of war against China has already brought very serious strain to Japan. What would be the strain against an industrially advanced and well-armed coalition?

Then there is the bogy of an "ideological bloc." I fancy you are not so frightened of that as some delegates at League meetings appeared to be, up to the January Council this year. Then the subject was dealt with rationally, for the first time, by no less a person than Mr. Anthony Eden, who admitted that the League has its own peculiar ideology, not as regards any particular system of government, but in respect of " peace through international co-operation." M. Delbos, who was then still French Foreign Minister, identified this ideology with " defending our conceptions of the relations between States, against the risks of international anarchy." In other words, a Peace Bloc for mutual assistance against aggressors would not be concerned with uniformity in methods of government. How could it, with semi-military dictatorships in it like Lithuania, Yugoslavia and Roumania, democratic republics like Czechoslovakia, Empires like the British and the French, a Socialist State like the U.S.S.R.? It would be concerned solely with respect for peace. The essential principles of that ideology, Litvinov pointed out in his speech, are " respect for the integrity and independence of all existing States, inviolability of their frontiers, renunciation of war as an instrument for settling international disputes, recognition of the equal rights of all peoples, great and small." Let anyone who objects to " ideological blocs " explain why such principles should not become the basis of an international alliance for mutual defence against the aggressor bloc, whose external policy is based on contempt for those principles!

Then there is the argument that " force—or the threat of force—proves nothing; there would still be the problem of the international injustices which the Fascist rulers exploit to win support." There is another version of this argument, would-be revolutionary in its form, but in reality most anti-revolutionary: " Nothing is of any use, so long as you haven't ended the capitalist system which breeds wars." I would not under any circumstances suggest that the successful formation of a Peace Bloc would usher in a ready-made system of international justice, still less that it would mean the end of the capitalist system. But can anyone doubt that the effect of a heavy rebuff on the strained machinery of the Fascist State, on the one hand, and the immense effort to rouse public opinion in such countries as Great Britain and France, on the other, which must be the necessary conditions for any successful Peace Bloc, will open the door to further advances towards social justice and international justice?

iv. *What Hinders the Building of a Peace Bloc?*

I think, in conclusion, that it would be useful to say something on what appear to be the obstacles to the formation of a Peace Bloc.

First, in my opinion, comes the responsibility of the National Government, which has so far chosen to throw the weight of the richest and most powerful Empire in the world into the scales on the side of the Fascists, instead of resistance to their aggression. Thereby it has frightened dozens of small peoples away from the cause of collective security. I do not suggest, after several examples I have quoted earlier, that various French Governments are entirely free from responsibility; but their extraordinary feeling of dependence on Great Britain—whether it is based on reality or not—has been the explanation of much of their passivity. The United States Government, which sent its delegation to the miserable Brussels Conference last November with the one watchword, so far as any of us could make out, not to do anything about Japanese aggression which might remotely involve the danger of war, also bears a share of responsibility; but its distance from Europe and European aggressors must not be forgotten. As for the Soviet Union, I really believe I cannot be charged with partiality when I say that it bears least responsibility of any for the present state of things. In the Ethiopian dispute, it offered to join in oil sanctions, and to stand by all the possible consequences, if Great Britain would do the same. I do not need to dwell on its record during the Spanish war. Wellington Koo declared at the League Council in May that only one Power had fulfilled its obligations to China under the Covenant, and everyone knew whom he meant. In March of this year, after the occupation of Austria and the Polish ultimatum to Lithuania, the Soviet Government sent a Note to Great Britain, France, the U.S.A. and Czechoslovakia, offering to begin the discussion—with States inside the League or outside—of practical measures to organise "collective action, aimed at stopping the further development of aggression, and eliminating the increased danger of a new world slaughter." The offer was declined as "not opportune" (in the words of the spokesmen of the National Government).

Why does the present British Government consider the organisation of collective resistance to existing and threatened aggression to be inopportune? That is a question which worries many people in many countries. Perhaps you will allow me to quote the reply which Litvinov gave to a similar question, at an election meeting in Leningrad on June 23 this year:

"In our time, unlike past centuries, wars are not waged alone by knights and feudal lords together with their menials, not alone by mercenary and professional armies. To-day the broadest masses of the people, entire peoples, are drawn into war. To win a victory in a serious conflict, tremendous sacrifices—the straining of all the forces of the people—are demanded; but in order to inspire the people to great deeds, to secure the necessary sacrifice from them, it is necessary to promise them something in the event of victory. We saw that after the world war the ruling classes in almost all countries had to extend the political rights of the workers and the petty bourgeoisie, and improve their economic position. The creation of the League of Nations was also, to a certain extent, a payment on promissory notes issued to the people during the war, in fulfilment of the slogan that that war would be the last war, that universal disarmament would be carried out and eternal peace guaranteed. These concessions were gradually taken back, the promises of disarmament and eternal peace remain unfulfilled. And now there arises the apprehension that after the new war the workers, peasants and petty bourgeoisie, taught by bitter experience, will defend the positions they have won with greater determination, and will not give them up. Further, there are not a few people among the ruling classes of western countries who naïvely believe that Fascism is really an enduring barrier against an advance by the working class. And inasmuch as the aggressor States are at the same time the bulwark of Fascism, there is the apprehension that a defeat of the aggressor States in a war, or even their diplomatic defeat, might prove to be a defeat for Fascism, and the destruction of this artificial dam against the labour movement. To this is added one more apprehension, that for the necessary balance in the struggle against the aggressor countries, co-operation with the Soviet Union will inevitably be required, and this, it appears, might also have an effect upon the international political struggle, adverse to the reactionary circles. Thus, it appears, these circles prefer to sacrifice their national interests, endanger and even lose their position as a State, for the sake of preserving their social and class positions. These are the kind of considerations that dictate the flabbiness and passivity of the foreign policy observed by us in certain foreign countries, the officiousness and submissiveness before the Fascist aggressors, which have resulted in the radical change in the correlation of forces in Europe and the entire world.

" . . . There are, of course, representatives and circles of the bourgeoisie which hold other views, which without renouncing their class privileges wish primarily to uphold their State interests, their national independence, their national and universal culture, who see in Fascism merely an ephemeral phenomenon. . . . Disputes in foreign policy occur mainly between those who uphold purely class interests, on the one hand, and the national patriotically-inclined elements, reflecting mainly the views of the petty bourgeoisie, the intelligentsia and the toilers, on the other."

If the ruling classes in the Fascist countries, which are also drawn from big business, appear on the surface to be less sensitive to the social consequences and risks of war, that is only because, so far, they have been pursuing successfully a policy of bluff and bullying, of attacks on weaker States—Litvinov pointed out—and not challenging a war on equal terms. In any case, " apart from adventures and gambles there is no policy that Fascism can pursue."

How Can the Aggressor be Stopped?

I believe the analysis I have just quoted to be the right one. All the actions, and many of the words, of the National Government, fit it like a glove.

But that being so, there is a second responsibility for the failure, so far, to throw up an effective barrier to this murderous threat to civilisation which is creeping over the world. It is the responsibility of those active minds who could lead the people (if they chose) in a campaign to change their national policy—not only in Great Britain—but who busy themselves instead with delusions. Some seek to salve their own consciences by utopian dreams of non-resistance, which Hitler himself might have invented to further his cause. Some seek an excuse for inaction in idle talk of "round-table conferences" and "frank talks"—as though it is argument and diplomatic contact with Hitler and Mussolini that are lacking. Some—and they are numerous—will not co-operate with A. or B., whatever their respective influence, energy or concern for peace, because they are sure that A. or B. will not help them to introduce Socialism by Act of Parliament after the next General Election.

In regard to that argument, I would make only this comment: that the very question they are begging is whether there is to be any next General Election for them to win, or any Parliament in which to legislate. It is surely more than a coincidence that the invasion of Spain began precisely as the reply to the unmistakeable verdict of a General Election, and the occupation of Austria was precipitated by the Austrian Chancellor's decision to hold a plebiscite. Or do they imagine that they can persuade Hitler and Mussolini to postpone a war, if the Fascist rulers decide on one, until after the next General Election?

No more useful work for international peace can be carried on, by those who have taken the trouble to inform themselves of international affairs, than to combat such theories of inaction among the people from whom they come, and to develop the fight for a Peace Bloc to resist and, if necessary, to crush the aggressor.

CHAPTER IX

THE VIEWPOINT OF THE SMALLER EUROPEAN STATES

by

HENRI ROLIN

Member of the Belgian Senate and formerly Legal Adviser to the Belgian Ministry of Foreign Affairs

i. *The Origin and Composition of the Oslo Group.*

THE title of my paper: "The Viewpoint of the Smaller European States," requires some preliminary explanations and reservations. What are the smaller European States? If it were my task to consider all the European States other than the Great Powers, to analyse the situation of Spain, the latest victim of the League crisis; of Poland, the sphinx; of Czechoslovakia, so tragically threatened by the extension of Germany on her southern frontier; of the other states of the Little Entente and of the Balkan Entente, influenced not only by the prestige of the dictators, but still more by the economic supremacy which the audacious policy of M. Schacht has gained for his country; I could not hope to expose in detail all these different situations. I shall limit myself therefore to one group of small European States, one which may be called the Oslo Group, representing some thirty million inhabitants, at first sight enjoying a much greater security than the countries I have mentioned, not nearly so well armed, yet having all together at least the economic importance of a great power and exercising a real influence on the activity of the League.

I must make a further reservation. I am not going to

speak as an official representative of Belgium on the point of view of these states. I have been legal adviser of the Belgian Government, but had to resign when I became a member of the Senate, and for the last two years I have not been a member of the Belgian delegation to the Assembly of the League. The reason for this is my declared antagonism towards the foreign policy of my Government. It is only fair to state this clearly so that you may be on your guard against personal bias, though, of course, I shall do my best to be as objective as possible, for I hold that, before discussing a point of view, one must try without any prejudice to understand its origins and development.

First of all, what was the origin of the Oslo Group and what were its first manifestations? At present the Oslo Group is composed of seven states: the four Scandinavian states, Sweden, Norway, Denmark and Finland, together with Holland, Belgium and Luxembourg. Though the group in its present form is of quite recent date and was in fact constituted in Copenhagen at the beginning of July, 1938, inside the group there still exists a much older nucleus composed of the four Scandinavian states. That Scandinavian group dates from the early days of the war. It was King Gustav of Sweden who took the initiative of calling his colleagues, the Kings of Norway and Denmark, together at a meeting in Malmo as early as 18th December, 1914. Their purpose was to deliberate upon the means of upholding neutrality and upon the decisions any of those Governments should take when difficulties arose. They met several times during the war. When the war was over, they thought it useful to continue the same contact for the adoption of a common attitude regarding the League. They had meetings nearly every year before each Assembly—18 in all. Since 1934 Finland has become a fourth member of the group. Leaving Finland aside, the first link between those states was their neutrality during the war. This qualification they shared with some other European States and very soon they found it useful to establish contact also with those other ex-neutrals inside the League. During the Peace Conference in 1919 there was in Paris a Conference of Neutrals which sent to the Committee of the Hôtel Crillon proposals of amendments to the Covenant and was allowed to participate in their discussion. In the first years of the Geneva institution there were other meetings of that larger group of ex-neutrals at which they compared their views and combined their efforts to lead the League in the directions they preferred.

One of their main preoccupations in those early years was to make the League universal and more especially to secure the admission of Germany as a member. Another was to achieve as soon as possible the general reduction of armaments prescribed in Article 8 of the Covenant and in wanting this they not only had in mind the suppression of the dangers arising from the inequality existing between Germany and the Allied Powers but also a genuine belief that without a general reduction of arms the exercise of a general coercion would prove too heavy for their countries. Concerning Article 16 of the Covenant, partly because of the dangers of war and partly because of their natural litany for the status of neutrality, they were genuinely reluctant to share the efforts made to develop and organise sanctions and shared the British view held at that time even by Lord Cecil that the strength of the League was essentially of a moral nature, that it had its foundations in a public opinion moulded by the publicity of its debates and so powerful that no one would dare to resist it.

With regard to the settlement of disputes on the other hand, the small powers of the north were very strong *legalists;* they did not trust the impartiality of the *political* bodies of the League—the Council and the Assembly. They wanted jurisdiction to be taken away from these bodies and the Covenant to be amended or developed so as to make arbitration obligatory at any rate in most cases. Finally, they insisted on the necessity of not limiting the activity of the League to political matters but of building up a real solidarity between the members of the League by a full application of the provisions of the Covenant referring to equal treatment of the different countries in matters of trade.

On the last two points Belgium was in full agreement with the group of neutrals, while at the same time she shared the views of France's allies—that the admission of Germany should be retarded, disarmament adjourned and Article 16 developed. On the whole, the position of the Belgian delegation was a kind of link between the ex-neutrals and the partisans of a stronger League.

ii. *The Turning Point: The Ethiopian Collapse.*

Yet there was a moment in the history of the League when all the different points of view seemed ready to unite for common action. That was when, in October, 1935, the Assembly decided to assist Ethiopia in resisting Italian aggression. It must be fully acknowledged that, all through that experiment of sanctions the attitude of the ex-neutrals was perfectly loyal. Already in August, 1935, one month before Sir Samuel Hoare's famous speech, the Scandinavian group, after a meeting in Oslo, had issued a communiqué according to which "they had assumed that this conflict would be dealt with in fullest harmony with the regulations of the Covenant and they would give their support to every effort to safeguard peace and maintain the principles of justice embodied in the Covenant." This keen attitude, contrasting with the hesitations shown in previous years, was certainly dictated by the feeling of the growing danger to peace resulting from the attitude of the dictators. Hitler had shown that he seriously meant to use the threat of war as a principal instrument of German policy. Mussolini boasted of the growth of Italy's strength. At that moment it appeared to everybody that the framers of the Covenant had been wise in inserting Articles 10 and 16 and that, unless the nations combined in their resistance, the world would again know a reign of violence and injustice.

The Dutch Minister for Foreign Affairs, M. de Graaf, after Sir Samuel Hoare's speech, declared in September, 1935, that his country knew that it would be involved in any new war that might break out in Europe. The Belgium Prime Minister, M. van Zeeland, promised that Belgium, true to her noblest traditions, would "be faithful to her obligations to the end."

Yet, from the very first, there were indications that the League would not go the whole way. Mr. Seton Watson in his recent book, *Britain and the Dictators,* reveals the fact that the day before Sir Samuel Hoare's speech the British minister and his French colleague agreed that the Suez Canal would remain open and that they would take no action which might lead to generalisation of the war. We have every reason to believe that Mussolini was informed of that secret decision. From that time he was the real master of the sanctions; he could get adjournment of any measure which would have too grave an effect on his military action simply by declaring that should it be applied he would resort to war. The ex-neutrals noted with surprise the obstruction of France and the complacent weakness of Great Britain which culminated in the Laval-Hoare proposal indignantly censured by the House of Commons. Public opinion in many countries at that time was so fully aware of the necessity of winning the victory for peace that quite certainly it would have supported the really drastic oil sanctions recommended by the experts in March, 1936. But at that time a German move, perhaps concerted with Italy, saved the situation of the latter. The reoccupation of German territory destroyed every tendency in Paris, London and Brussels to impose the will of the League on Mussolini. While the British Government advised the French not to take any military action it at the same time had the naïvity to invite the Italian Government to participate in the deliberations of London. This was the fatal blow to the League. The other sanctionist powers looked with dismay on the attempt of the Locarno powers to reconcile the aggressor state. Even when Ethiopian resistance had been broken by the use of gases on a large scale, the Danish and Dutch Governments openly declared that they could see no reason why sanctions should be lifted.

There was a moment of hope when the Socialist leaders, M. Leon Blum, formed his Government in France, but this was so preoccupied with social reforms and so anxious to rebuild Anglo-French friendship endangered by

M. Laval that it allowed Great Britain to understand that Paris was ready to agree to anything which might be proposed one way or the other. So it came about that the Assembly met in July, 1936, with the formal proposal to lift the sanctions to which British diplomacy had already won so many adhesions. The debates of that Assembly show how deeply many countries resented what might be called the treachery of the Locarno powers. It is worth noting that, even after the acceptance of this proposal, when a vote was taken on Ethiopia's request for financial assistance to carry on the fight for its independence, only a minority of the Assembly voted against the proposal, the majority abstaining in order to leave responsibility for that decision with the Locarno powers.

iii. *Policy of the Oslo Group After the Failure of Sanctions.*

The bitter conclusion drawn from the sanctions experiment by the ex-neutrals was expressed in their collective note of 1st July, 1936, which said that so long as the Covenant as a whole was not applied consistently those states would have to take account of that fact in their execution of the Covenant of the League.

The gravity of that note was not felt until some time later. At first it was regarded merely as a sort of censure on the states that had taken the lead in the institution and the abandonment of sanctions but when the reform of the League was discussed in the Committee of Twenty-eight the Swedish delegate, Mr. Unden, very clearly indicated that, in the opinion of his Government, in view of the attitude of the Great Powers, the binding force of Article 16 was suspended and that the Swedish Government would act in conformity with that opinion pending the conclusion of the Committee. The Copenhagen Declaration of July, 1938, to which the Belgian Government has also agreed went further, it simply denied the binding force of Article 16, irrespective of any decision which might be taken on the point by the bodies of the League.

Of course, some of the Ministers present at the meeting insisted at the time or in later declarations that they remained faithful to the idea of collective security, underlining that their Government still reserved the option of joining in collective action. In this they differed very clearly from the attitude of permanent neutrality adopted by Switzerland, but in reality one must confess that the difference is rather theoretical and that there is no great hope that, in the event of a new conflict, anything is to be expected of those Governments. Indeed we see that in October, 1937, the Scandinavian delegates present in Brussels abstained from voting the very weak resolution moved by that Conference; they gave as their reason that their country had no great interest in the Far East. If we remember that at the same time they have declared themselves very anxious not to run any risk of war by the application of sanctions, which means that they would probably also abstain in the case of a conflict interesting a neighbour state, we are led to doubt whether there is any possible case in which those Governments would be ready to intervene. May we add that at least one of those Governments—the Danish—does not conceal its preference for neutrality in all cases. The Congress of the International Federation of League of Nations Societies had the occasion last July to listen to a very interesting lecture by M. Cohn, legal adviser to the Danish Foreign Office, in which neutrality was represented as much superior to collective security because it means a fight against war itself and not against only one of the belligerents—the so-called aggressor state. . . .

iv. *The Attitude of Belgium.*

But how are we to explain the Belgian Government's adhesion to that Declaration? It is in fact the last step of two years' evolution which began with the denunciation of Locarno made known to the world in a somewhat unusual way—the publication of a speech of King Leopold III to his Ministers in October, 1936. The reasons for this first step were clear—a feeling of the growing danger on our Eastern frontier had led the King and the Government to the conviction that the Belgian army must be strengthened. This necessitated increased expenditure and longer military service. Any proposals in that direction were sure to meet with resistance, especially from the side of the Flemish population and it was felt that the Flemish national party would try to explain the military proposals as a consequence of our commitments to France. It was necessary therefore to denounce not only the military agreement with France but also that part of the Locarno Treaty which seemed to imply in cases of German aggression against France the military co-operation of Belgium for the protection of France. Those reasons were explained to the French and British Governments whose agreement was obtained for the denunciation. But there was still Article 16 with the obligation to allow a passage through our territory to the troops of members of the League taking part in common action against an aggressor. The King's speech seemed simply to ignore that obligation of Belgium under the Covenant. The point was raised in the Belgian Parliament. Discussions took place, and in the end the attitude of the Belgian Foreign Office was revealed to be on these lines: that, while acknowledging the full obligatory character of the economic sanctions, the exercise of the right of passage for troops would depend on Belgian acknowledgement that the passage requested was justified by the necessities of real common action against a real aggression.

Now it is clear that the Belgian adhesion to the Copenhagen Declaration has quite another meaning. It no longer lays stress on the qualification of our obligation but simply denies its existence and this not only with regard to the right of passage but also with regard to economic sanctions.

If you ask my opinion regarding that policy, I must before making any criticism state the facts that determined it. It is quite true that when one considers the text of Article 16 along with the present map of the world one must acknowledge that an integral and automatic execution of sanctions would in some cases lead to no result at all. We must not forget that the German-Italian-Japanese block is not only a political block but in part a geographical one. Since the *Anschluss* Germany and Italy form one continuous territory with great material resources dividing Europe in two. Economic sanctions exercised generally against such a block would probably in many cases cause greater harm to the sanctionist states than to the aggressor. But the Covenant does not impose such a quixotic execution of its provisions. The obligations must be interpreted in view of their effect and if loyal examination proves that some of them in some cases are useless or even harmful for the purpose contemplated, the League will not be weakened by recognising the fact. To that extent the attitude of the Oslo Group seems justified.

v. *Weaknesses of the Copenhagen Policy.*

My criticism of the Copenhagen policy is firstly : that there is in it an element of unreality : when some of the Ministers who signed the Declaration state that they still have the right to intervene in some cases, I believe, as I have already indicated, that in practice they will never make use of that right. But I would add that, even if I am mistaken in that conclusion, by making the execution of sanctions optional and uncertain, sanctions are deprived of what was their greatest merit—the preventive effect which the fear of them if certain to be applied, might exercise on an aggressor state.

My chief criticism is that, even from the narrow point of view which these states adopt, that of the immediate national interest, the Copenhagen policy does not tend to increase their security or to diminish their risks. Denmark, whose Government professes a sort of blind faith in security as though the dangers of war could be averted by auto-suggestion—makes a strange mistake in forgetting that part of her present territory is due to the victory of the Allies and that, as one of her deputies recalled in parliament a few months ago, it might well happen that Hitler, in one of his moods, would think of forcibly imposing the return of that territory to Germany. Even more is this the case for Belgium. Not only has this country also won a part of her territory in the war of 1914-1918 under circumstances which have sometimes been criticised, but it has a colony. And if, judging from experience, Belgium may reasonably rely on French and British assistance for the defence of its independence, perhaps even of the integrity of its territory, certainly those big states have not the same interest in leaving the Congo or the mandated territory under Belgian rule. On the contrary, once the principles of right are abandoned, there might be a temptation to look in that direction for a solution of the colonial problem. And yet Belgium's greatest danger lies not in her possession of Eupen-Malmédy or colonial territories, but in her geographical position. It is a historical fact that, when Germany and France are at war, the stronger army has an interest in extending the front on the German-French frontier to the north and making use of Belgium's good roads. Possibly, in some event of war, Germany would not find this to her advantage at the outset but, on the contrary, would want to use the main bulk of her armies against some state in the east or south, *e.g.* Czechoslovakia. It is possible too that France would hesitate to impose on us, even with the approval of Great Britain and of many members of the League, the respect of the right of passage for troops taking part in a common action to rescue Czechoslovakia. But what would be the consequence? Most probably this—that it being made more difficult for France to intervene successfully, it would be made possible for Germany to crush Czechoslovakia. And then the second act of the drama would open, in which the interests of the German army would certainly, as in 1914, ignore the little scrap of paper of the new Belgian neutrality. Then we should know the dangers and horrors which we have tried to escape. But, worse than that, we should have made victory more doubtful and we should run the greater risk of having contributed by our negative attitude to the triumph of militarism and dictatorship in Europe.

vi. *Conclusions.*

My conclusion can be brief. I hope that the Copenhagen Declaration will meet with opposition both inside my country and outside. When Switzerland obtained from the Council of the League its consent to her return to integral neutrality, the necessity of that consent was expressly stressed in the Council's resolution. No such consent has been asked by the states of Copenhagen and, for my part, I cannot accept the opinion that, in these circumstances, they have juridically put an end to their obligations.

Some of you may be surprised that a Belgian citizen takes a position in this way against his own Government but, as I have tried to show, in doing so I have the full conviction that I am serving not only the cause of peace and justice but also the real interests of my country.

CHAPTER X

THE IDEOLOGICAL CONFLICT

by

E. F. CARRITT

Fellow of University College, Oxford, University Lecturer in Philosophy

i. *National Allegiance and International Relations.*

THE Ideological Conflict is the subject given to me, but the word ideology is one from which, as Dr. Johnson said, the human mind naturally retires. I am told it was invented by Napoleon. All the phrases of dictators are, I think, apt to convey rather more heat than light, although I should except from that the very bright remark of Mussolini that "The man who declares war is not the man who signs the peace treaty." Since, then, I do not know what I ought to be doing, I must do the only thing I can do. That is I must try to tell you what I think the connection is between the papers on international relations and my own studies. That line of study is sometimes called political philosophy but even the word philosophy is perhaps one from which the mind shies. I prefer to call it the theory of obedience or the theory of political obligation. It is an attempt to answer the question: Why ought we to obey? or Whom ought we to obey? That has sometimes been narrowed down to the form: Why ought we to obey our country's government? or Who would constitute such a government as we really ought to obey? But, when it is so stated, the question, of course, is really begged, because it has been assumed that our allegiance or obedience to anybody is due always and only, in the last resort, to our country's government. But plainly loyalties are divided. I may owe some obedience to my parents, to a church, to a university, to a trade union, some to my country and so on, and these can conflict.

It is hardly necessary perhaps to emphasise that the question is not: Whom *do* I obey? I may obey a policeman or a gangster through fear, or a customer through hope of profit. Even the proper question: Whom ought I to obey? is very often quite uninteresting because, if my parents tell me to obey the law and the law tells me to obey my parents and if I happen to want that, no question really arises. The problem of political obligation arises when I am commanded to do something which I do not want to do and which I should even think it wrong to do if I had not been so commanded. And yet it is clear that we sometimes think we ought to obey a law which we believe to be both inconvenient to ourselves and unjust or pernicious to others. I had American friends who thought prohibition absurd and dangerous, but they held that, while it was in force, they ought to conform; and I am inclined to think they were right.

The bearing of all this on international relations is clear. Is there or could there be any international or collective power which might properly share or dispute my allegiance to my country, as my country properly shares my allegiance to my parents? Could there be a power which I sometimes ought to obey to my own and to my country's disadvantage and even when I thought its commands unjust? The answers which people give to this question will depend a good deal on the view they take of their allegiances to their own country, and to some extent on their political philosophy. I am very far from wishing to exaggerate the influence of philosophy on a man's politics, either for good or evil. In both directions *on peut toujours faire des accommodements avec son ciel Philosophique.* Philosophical hedonists are very often self-sacrificing people, utilitarians just, and Kantians opportunist, and they are all capable of the most desperate sophisms to reconcile their theory and practice. I regard as pernicious nonsense the doctrine that you cannot be socialist unless you are a dialectical materialist or that if you are you must be. I think an idealist or an agnostic might be a perfectly good socialist. And, just because men can always thus interpret their theories to fit their practice, we should refuse to co-operate with nobody on purely ideological grounds. " By their fruits ye shall know them " is the right maxim both for toleration in dogma and for democratic freedom of thought. But also, for the very same reason—because men do thus interpret their metaphysical theories to justify their conduct—these interpretations which they make are symptomatic to some extent of the way they mean to behave, and cannot altogether be neglected. People do try to rationalise their conduct by philosophies. And after all the best thing about men in the mass is that they are hypocrites. That is perhaps the most obvious achievement of Christianity. We may not be much more just or much more unselfish than our predecessors but, if we can judge by Thucydides and Machiavelli, I think we are a little less shameless. Tyrants nowadays are always the saviours of their people, imperialist conquerors gratuitously carry the white man's burden, profiteers are captains of industry. And so these interpretations which men or nations make of their philosophical tradition, and perhaps to some slight extent even the nature of the tradition they accept in political philosophy, may give us some sort of inkling of the way they mean to behave.

I want then to say something about the main theories of political obligation which have been held and to ask what bearing these, or the interpretations men have put upon them, have on international relations. Of course, I must state matters very roughly. I must dispense with qualifications and quotations that I should like to give. There are, I think, five traditional reasons which have been given why we should very often obey our Government even when we think it wrong. Attempts have also been made to combine two or more of these. It is an attempt to combine two of them which I myself adopt.

ii. *Theories of Allegiance* (a) *Self-interest.*

The first answer we can dismiss at once, because it is not a reason why we ought to obey but why we very often do obey and nearly always would if we were quite prudent and selfish. It was the answer given by some of the Greek philosophers and by Hobbes: *It pays.* So long as the holders of power do hold power and provide some kind of order and security, any degree of slavery to them is pleasanter than the risks of revolution and anarchy. The corollary of that theory for international relations is clear. International anarchy makes human life pretty well as nasty, brutish and short as does internal anarchy, if only people were wise enough to see it. They would always be wise to obey an international sovereign. But is there any power or force which will, even if irksome and damaging to ourselves, be a sure refuge from international anarchy? The answer to those whose practice as well as their theory is founded on self-interest is clear. We must *make* it their interest and their obvious interest to look for security only in collective security.

(b) *Contract or Consent.*

But, secondly, perhaps not so many people are actuated by sheer self-interest as have professed it though perhaps some who are do not profess it; so this theory has generally been masked by being somewhat inconsistently confused with another theory, that of the Contract. On this view, men, recognising the inconvenience of their natural state of warfare, get together and for mutual advantage make a compact, either with one another to set up a ruler whom all should obey, or with some powerful individual to obey him in return for protection and security. There are two obvious objections to that theory. The first is that there is precious little evidence for such foundation of states and much for their foundation in other ways, and the second is that we should not be bound by the contracts of our remote ancestors. And these objections to the theory have compelled its defenders to resort to the device of what they call a tacit contract supposed to be made by every man, perhaps when he comes of age, or perhaps as soon as he consciously accepts any benefit and protection from the society. This is not very plausible; and, as it is not a very influential doctrine to-day, perhaps we need not spend long on it. The most respectable form of the theory founds itself on what is called government by consent. The suggestion is that, even a minority, by voting, has undertaken to abide by the result of the vote, as, if a man plays pitch and toss, presumably he undertakes to pay if he loses. The analogy, as you see at once, is not fair. I can toss or not, but nobody asks me whether I will vote for my governors or govern myself. No doubt it is true that in elections it is "Heads I win, tails you win," but it is also, "If you don't play, you lose." Before leaving the contract theory we might note its implications for international relations. Even if states have not been founded by contract, federations and alliances for arbitration and collective security may be and have been. There would be the same interest in making such contracts and the same obligation to keep them as with contracts to set up a state, and if we owe anything in the way of gratitude to our state, we do not owe less to humanity; so it is very difficult to see how anyone who founded his patriotic loyalty on this ground could refuse a wider allegiance.

(c) *The General Will.*

The third theory is the one which has, I think, for the last 150 years had the greatest influence—not a very direct one, but philosophies do have an indirect influence—that is the theory of what is called the General Will. As you know no doubt, it is to be found in a confused and rudimentary form in Rousseau, was elaborately formulated by Hegel and has been clearly presented to English readers by Bosanquet in his *Philosophical Theory of the State*. It is very difficult in a short space to state fairly a theory so elusive, if one has little sympathy with it. But I must try. When men unite for some common end, there comes into being a supernatural entity called the general or real will which is neither the will of any one of them, nor or all of them, nor of the majority of them. Nor is it a metaphorical fiction. It is said to be real, more real than the wills of any individuals, which compared with it are mere whims, errors, illusions. It is said that the wills of the individuals are unreal as compared with the general will, somewhat as my dreams or passing fancies might metaphorically be called unreal as compared with my fixed rational policy of life. Being more real, it is said to be better, and to it ought to be subordinated not only the desires but also the consciences of all members of the society. It is not manifested in their votes or their convictions but in the laws, in the institutions, in the customs, in the " spirit " of the country. I do not see any reason to believe any of this. Why there should be a general will any more than a general belief, a general memory, a general pain or anger, a general taste or general sense of humour, I cannot conceive. If I did believe it, I think I should go on to conjecture that there must be a general will of humanity for the good of the race, as far superior to any national will as that is alleged to be to mind. Rousseau in the *Economie Politique,* though not in the *Contrat Social,* just suggests this possibility and Bosanquet hinted it once; Hegel I think never, mainly I suppose because he despised moral facts which had not yet got physical power to enforce themselves. Although he prided himself on being the philosopher of history and of development he constantly falls into the blunder of accepting the actual of his time as the final and ultimate, as what he would himself call the real or the rational. In fact this theory, at least since Fichte, has been interpreted, I think, almost entirely in a nationalist, imperialist and indeed totalitarian sense, with the possible exception, which I will mention later, of Marxism. Hegel held that states could have no obligations either to one another or to their own members. The power and aggrandisment of the state are the sole criteria of good and evil. The state can do no wrong. The state is God walking upon earth. Might is right. It is " hussars with shining sabres " who introduce the kingdom of heaven.

I am not persuaded that there are any general wills or, if there were, that they must be national wills and that they would have no obligations to other national wills. If the holders of this theory are consistent, they must hold that a state should make alliances, treaties, leagues, when it can gain anything by so doing and break them when it can gain by that. It is a little odd that such a general will should ever wish to publish its own immorality, since complete untrustworthiness can hardly be a national asset. Perhaps besides the general will this is a general naïveté.

(d) *Utilitarianism.*

The fourth reason offered why we ought to obey our government is the purely utilitarian one. This neither looks backward to some past contract nor does it invoke any metaphysical entity. It asserts that we have a duty to our fellow men, one duty which is always the same : to produce the greatest possible amount of happiness in the circumstances. And at least ninety-nine times out of a hundred we shall cause more misery by rebellion, leading to civil war, than by obedience coupled with an effort to reform the law constitutionally. Even open disobedience or passive defiance is harmful by causing disrespect for law and order. That was the view of my American friends about prohibition. The implication of this theory for inter-state relations is clear. Utilitarianism by its very nature is internationalism. Patriotism and loyalty can only be justified as they serve the happiness of all mankind. This theory is opposed to the first three. Our allegiance to our government depends no longer upon its usefulness to ourselves personally either in the future or the past, as it did on the selfish and contract theories, nor yet upon its power to aggrandise our state, as with the general will, but upon its services to humanity. The more we think that our country's government and constitution and influence are serviceable to the world, the more we should feel bound to do nothing that would in any way weaken it, even while we try to amend its errors. So soon as we came to think that its efforts were exerted for a merely selfish patriotism, careless of the welfare of subject races or of other nations, then our allegiance would *ipso facto* disappear. It would have no moral claim on us whatever. What has such a claim on us is any power willing and able to increase the prosperity and happiness of the world. I do not see how anyone holding the utilitarian theory could refuse allegiance to any practicable method of ending war, or how it could give allegiance to any government capable of aggression or of preferring war to arbitration.

(e) *Natural Rights.*

The fifth and last type of political philosophy is sometimes called the Natural Rights theory. This holds that governmental machinery is not perhaps competent to do very much in the way of making its subjects happy, and that certainly that is not its first or only duty, if it is its duty at all. Its main function is to secure justice; to defend every man's life, freedom and property—by property being understood what he has earned. No doubt these things are important conditions of happiness, but the emphasis laid by this theory is rather on the *right* to freedom of speech, to equality of opportunity, to equality of distribution for their own sakes; whereas for a theory intent only on the sum-total of happiness, equality is a matter of indifference. Utilitarianism must always be ready to sacrifice the innocent to the majority but justice might not. For myself, I would just say in passing that I think the only satisfactory formula for political obligation is a combination of these last two: utilitarianism and natural rights. I think our allegiance is due to any established power, and it is our duty to establish any power, in proportion as it is likely to increase the happiness of the world and also to promote justice—that is, the merited distribution of freedom, power, and opportunity for happiness and self development. I do not think either the promotion of happiness or the promotion of justice by itself can cover all our duties. I think we have one duty to make the world happier and another to distribute that happiness in accordance with man's just claims.

Here again, on the natural rights theory, the consequences for international relations are not obscure. Anyone who believes in justice and the right of every man, irrespective of nationality, to equal opportunities for happiness and self-development, anyone who believes in the right of freedom of thought and of speech, in economic and legal equality, cannot easily think that these rights are best left to the arbitrament of sheer force, which is no more likely to give just decisions than the toss of a penny. He must believe that, however fallible human judges are, however difficult or impossible it is for them to be disinterested, yet a decision by argument and arbitration is less ridiculous than one by bombardment. Just as we owe obedience to our government's laws even if they are bad, so long as we believe that on the whole that government's authority is a guarantee of more justice and less violence than would be brought about by our violent resistance, so, even if the settlements made by some collective system seem unjust, it is our duty to abide by them and to enforce them rather than to weaken or discredit that system, unless we are quite certain of replacing it by some better alternative to violence.

This last theory, which bases political obligation on justice, is in the main the one put forward both by Locke in his *Essay on Civil Government* and by Kant, who was one of the earliest great writers to outline a scheme for a league of nations in his work *Perpetual Peace*.* Kant holds that the most pressing duty and the most difficult problem of the human race is the formation of a civil society, universally enforcing justice by laws. And not only, he says, is it a duty to attempt the solution of the problem but it is an attempt we may hope will be successfully carried out because the very existence of the race depends upon it. As the nasty and short brutality of individual life in a primitive state of lawlessness forced man to form national governments if he was to exist at all, so the miseries of war and the burden of armaments will force nations into collective security even against their will. This suggestion of his, of course, is the same sort of argument as that used by Marxists. It is "this or nothing." And it is also a synthesis of opposition.

* Translated by Hastie in *Kant's Principles of Politics* (Clark, Edinburgh, 1891).

iii. *Domestic Policy and International Relations.*

Kant also makes a significant point, that justice in the internal government of states and justice in their external relations are intimately bound up and mutually interdependent. One can hardly exist without the other. Wars lead to domestic disorder and, on the other hand, inequality and injustice at home lead to wars. Where force and interest rule at home they will probably also direct foreign policy. Conversely, those who coerce their dependencies or their neighbours will be unapt to encourage free discussion among themselves. I think it is a matter of history that in periods and peoples of the patriarchal stage, where family despotism is most unquestioned and severe, insubordination to a wider authority is most frequent. The domestic tyrant is not a good member of a club. Aggression only begins at home.

Among his other strikingly modern thoughts Kant suggests that peace is best preserved when the decision of peace or war rests with the people, because it is the people who suffer more than the rulers from war. He actually asserts that peace founded on a collective judicial system, backed by force, could only be ensured between republican nations, where every citizen is represented in the decision and where it is law that rules. He goes on, however, to distinguish a republic strongly if not very clearly from a democracy. He wants to make the distinction because he is afraid in democracies of the tyranny of the majority, which might deny the rights of freedom to some religious, racial or class minority. That is a charge brought against some democracies to-day—I do not know whether fairly or not—for instance against the Province of Quebec and the Republic of Eire, and also against all capitalist democracies in a different sense. Kant goes on to speak of what he calls the " Palladium of Liberty," which is not, as we might expect, universal franchise, but freedom of speech. That is a view which has been developed in a very interesting way by the Master of Balliol.*

This brings me to my last point : the brief application of these abstract theories to a concrete world situation. We have asked what are the implications of each of these theories for international relations. It remains to ask how far each of them is appropriate to the various forms of government we see about us : democracy, plutocracy, dictatorship. But before I do that, may I repeat my warning against expecting men to act consistently with their theories? We are not consistent animals.

To begin with I am afraid that, however much we might like, we cannot accept Kant's belief that peace is secured when the decision rests with the people. No doubt it would be if the people were wise, but they are even more liable than an oligarchy to the infection of mob passion. Let me quote the opinion of a newspaper which will hardly be suspected of aristocratic leanings : *The Daily Worker,* on the 4th of this month :†

> " On this day 24 years ago, hysterical crowds, misled by demagogic orators, deceived by a coldly calculating press, cheered the news that British troops were marching to kill and be killed."

The natural pacifism of democracies can be seduced by specious propaganda as well as violated by coercive militarism. The only defence—there is no absolute

* A. D. Lindsay, *The Essentials of Democracy.*
† August, 1938.

defence of course—against such propaganda is complete, real freedom of criticism, however much opposed to the government and however much opposed to public opinion; freedom in speech, freedom in writing, in education, in the press, in parliament, on the wireless, everywhere. I think that those nations where there is most freedom of speech, where domestic differences are settled by discussion rather than by discipline, are the ones most inclined for peaceful settlement of international questions. They are accustomed to obey their own government even when they think it wrong, because they see that on the whole a government which allows free discussion is more likely to promote or to allow prosperity and justice than any they can set up by sheer force; and so they will be prepared to abide by international arbitration, even when it seems manifestly unjust, because they see that such a method on the whole makes more for happiness and justice than ordeal by battle. Judges make plenty of mistakes and all judges are prejudiced, but they are still more like judges than bombs are. The laws delays are better than a quick-shooter, and though we know the law is an ass, we also know a live ass is better than a dead lion.

We saw that the political theory most hard to reconcile with orderly international relations was that of the general will, and we saw that this theory has been aptly adopted by totalitarian states with imperialist ambitions. It was indeed popular in our own country in the latter part of the last century, which was one of our most imperialist epochs. What is worse is that since Hegel's day, nationalism has become an even straiter creed. The real will was at least supposed to be somehow manifested in all members of the state community, but now it is a sort of physical nostrum and a bogus nostrum at that. It is confined to the seed of Abraham—or rather of the Aryans. With this new fundamentalism has come a severing of all the international arteries: literature, religion, science; they must now all be national and racial or they must be suppressed. Even foreign travel is minimised. I suppose there must be in certain European countries to-day a larger proportion of influential and well-educated people such as teachers who have never been abroad than at any time for the last 200 years.

Democracy, on the other hand—if that means majority rule—has generally been based on utilitarianism, I suppose on the assumption that what most people want and vote for is most likely to be for the greatest happiness of the greatest number. But about that we have seen that there are difficulties. The majority, though it always wants its own happiness is very easily misled. But if, as I have been trying to suggest, democracy is perhaps really more akin to what Kant called republicanism, that is to say if its essential is not so much majority rule as the ideal of equal economic and educational opportunity with complete freedom of criticism and opinion, and if universal suffrage is only regarded as a very good device, perhaps the best device, for minimising intolerance, then such democracy is best based on the natural rights theory; and that is also perhaps the most acceptable basis to Socialism so far as Socialism is a moral ideal as well as an economic expedient—though Socialism might also found itself on the greatest happiness of the greatest number.

If Communism is to be distinguished from Socialism, to which of the theories we have been enumerating is it best assigned? Marxism has, of course, its own official philosophy, if I may use such a contradiction in terms. It has borrowed from Hegel the idea of a general will though it does not use that term, a general will which overrides and should override the wills of individuals. But it identifies this will, not with the national state, but with the working class as the instrument of economic determinism. Thus it is essentially international and, so far, it certainly should welcome the peaceful settlement of international relations. Further it has borrowed from the utilitarian theory the aim of increasing the happiness of the mass of mankind, not of any privileged class; so it abjures imperialist exploitation and ambitions. But, on the other hand, Marxist theory despairs of overcoming the entrenched power of such interests without the use of force. It proclaims therefore a dictatorship, though a dictatorship of the proletariat which, like all modern dictatorships, claims to be exercised for the happiness of the majority and claims this more plausibly than most because it has divorced itself from the capitalist interest. But it does not think you can keep that interest at bay without establishing a totalitarian régime with a rigorous censorship of education, speech and press. Whether it is right or not in doing so, I do not pretend to say, but the effect on international relations is that a Marxist nation is in an ambiguous position, as perhaps all existing states are, because none of them have an ideal form of government. Part of its ideology (blessed word!) commits it to inter-nationalism and to anti-imperialism, but another part tends to the use of force rather than to argument and compromise. If a Communist state should avow the intention of imposing Communism upon democracies whose majority were unwilling to accept it, whether they would be right or wrong in so proposing I do not say, but it must be impossible for those democracies to expect from it the peaceful arbitration of all disputes. Just as, conversely, if a non-Communist state should avow the intention of wrecking Communism in a state that accepts it, then the Communists could not expect the peaceful settlement of international disputes from that other state.

I suggested that there is a similar ambiguity in our democracy. Its habits of government by vote and of free discussion should make it anti-militarist, and prepared for peaceful settlements, but its economic inequalities put great power into hands whose interests are by no means always peaceful. I suppose the ideal members of a comity of nations would be peoples completely democratic and completely socialised, with absolute freedom of speech and absolute economic equality. They would then be both habituated to government by discussion and vote and also freed from profit-making motives, imperialist ambitions and sinister alliances. But perhaps that is only to say that when we have the Kingdom of Heaven upon earth we shall have no more wars, or perhaps it is only to say that democracy cannot attain its ideals without economic equality and that Socialism necessarily returns towards democracy if its ideals are to be retained.

iv. *Summary.*

I said I find two reasons for obeying either my own or a world authority : the first so far as it promotes happiness, the second so far as it promotes justice. The first answers roughly to economic welfare and security and to the utilitarian theory : the second answers roughly to freedom and equality and to the natural rights theory. Correspondingly, I think there are two qualities in states which incline them to peaceful international relations : Socialist economy and freedom.

It seems to me that in Europe to-day we find three main ideologies. One is the confessedly selfish, if mystical, nationalism which regards any talk of international justice as mere sentimentality. The other two are opposed to it but apt to differ between themselves. The first of these is prepared to impose by force settlements which it honestly believes to be just and to resist by force all others; the other is prepared to accept and even to enforce almost any settlements reached by any process of open and free discussion, believing that all who accept such methods are in a way which will ultimately lead to more justice and happiness than will the imposition of our own ideals.

May I sum up the point I have tried to make by saying, that for the possibility of just international relations and peace, majority rule is something like a good engine, a very useful thing to have, because it probably makes the best use of your petrol—or perhaps I ought in this audience to say "gas." But the thing you *must* have, the thing without which engines, good or bad, are quite useless, is the gas—and that, as we all know, is the name given by dictators to government by discussion. But you cannot have real, effective freedom of speech, you cannot have freedom from interested and subsidised propaganda without economic equality. Do not misunderstand me. I do not like freedom of speech, nobody does, except his own. I am not looking forward to the criticisms of this paper, but I am quite certain there exists a Natural Right to make them; and perhaps after all I should prefer them to a free fight.

CHAPTER XI

REFUGEES—A PERMANENT PROBLEM IN INTERNATIONAL ORGANISATION

by

S. LAWFORD CHILDS

Of the International Labour Office

i. *No Provision for Refugees in the Covenant.*

THE Covenant of the League of Nations and the Constitution of the International Labour Organisation contain *specific* references not only to the great ameliorative processes and the improved international methods by which they proposed to eliminate war, dignify peace, and uplift humanity, but included also special mention (one might almost describe them as warrants for the arrest) of certain well recognised and old-established international public enemies, such, for example, as opium, epidemics, the traffic in women and children—and in munitions—all flourishing gangsters whose fingerprints and nefarious activities had figured for decades in the police gazettes of the world.

But there was no charter for political refugees, no solace for exiles.

Minorities, their cousins-germane, exploited workers, their brothers in affliction, migrants and native labourers, "writ with them in sour misfortune's book," all these are mentioned, but there is nothing about Stateless persons or *heimatlose*. Much may be found about the right of workers to associate, but there is nothing about the right of asylum. Unlike the churches of the Middle Ages, the original designs for the temple of peace provided for no sanctuary about the altar.

This notable omission by the peace-writers was a cause of real difficulty in after years to those who, in Geneva and elsewhere, were struggling to persuade the pundits, the pontiffs, and the Pontius Pilates of the international world and the over-Treasury minded in general, that international assistance for refugees was as proper a function of the League as, for example, the celebration of international conferences destined to free the world trade in hides, skins, and bones from the hampering restrictions that beset it and that refugee problems were likely to be as permanent as the poor who are " always with us." It also provided a good exit for those who had other reasons for deprecating international discussions about refugees.

" There is nothing in the Pact about refugees," the henchmen of hegemony would murmur apologetically to Dr. Nansen when he besought them in the corridors for more money for his work; and when he pressed them, as he always did, they would say that their Governments were rather uneasy about the whole question and that Dr. Nansen must excuse them, as they were due for an important session to consider the experts' report on the work of the sub-committee on phytopathological questions. The epidemic among the elm trees in Europe which was decimating the number of trees available for coffins and other purposes, including armaments,—there, they declared, was a serious matter, which required their attention, and it was, moreover, a direct result of the War, for during the terrible bombardments the wounds in the trees had caused the appearance of various new forms of fungoid growth, which, in their turn, had harboured the parasites which were killing the trees in defiance of the efforts of the experts to deal with them.

As for refugees—well, perhaps if Dr. Nansen could promise an immediate, cheap, and efficient scheme for transferring all the refugees which were a charge on their countries to the territories of somebody else, they would see what they could do to make their Government agree the credits.

Perhaps the most characteristic effect of this omission in the Pact and in the Constitution of the I.L.O. was the continual insistence by the Assembly that the refugee work of the League must be " liquidated " with the utmost rapidity and with a quarter of the resources which were available for parallel and equally insoluble problems which were allowed to meander peacefully through preliminary advisory committees, expert conferences and the like, towards the gentle adumbration of partial solutions.

The use of this word " liquidation " is the *leitmotif* of all the resolutions and decisions in the international world concerning the work for the refugees. It was a curious word, and its general use was brought about by general agreement often based on agreed misunderstanding. For by those who considered the situation of the refugees as tragic and worthy of international assistance it was regarded as indicating the necessity of terminating their sad position as soon as possible. For those on the other hand who disapproved of refugee work being done by the League at all, the word was regarded as denoting a decision to cease such work as soon as possible.

A great deal of confusion has resulted from this reliance of opposite opinion on differing interpretation.

Another factor which made for difficulty and inefficiency

was the conflict which grew up between two opposing schools of thought regarding what the League should try to do for refugees. Should it go in for direct operations, buy food, charter ships and so on itself, or should it merely stimulate and co-ordinate other agencies regarding this sort of action.

This is a very difficult question. The man in the street is in favour of the first alternative, for it answers his question " What has the League Done for Refugees? " in a definite and convincing way. Other and more complicated minds deny that direct action of that sort is the proper role of the League.

Just, they say, as the Labour Office is not itself an employment agency, but does its best to diminish unemployment through its conventions and in other ways, and seeing that you cannot get cured at the Hygiene Section or get a loan from the Financial Committee, so the Refugee Section should not itself feed the starving or clothe the naked.

This is a very difficult question. International administrative action or International Executive action? My own view is that there should be international machinery for both activities. Whether the same machine performs them both must be a question of expediency.

The general indecision about what really ought to be the precise function of the League and the Labour Office as regards the work for refugees—and it is a very difficult subject to be dogmatic about in view of the fact of sovereignty—led to a number of hesitations, difficulties and defects in action which have been criticised by various speakers and observers of the situation.

It resulted in the refugee services having a sort of

Cinderella status, and this again led to a great deal of their time being taken up in waging desperate battles for the continuation of their own existence, which, very naturally, diminished their efficiency and the amount of effort available for the real job they had in hand. It also had another deleterious effect. Faced as they were with the dilemma of either producing miraculous solutions—with insufficient resources—for situations for which nothing but palliatives could really be devised, or of seeing their administrative credits and executive funds diminish and finally disappear, they were subject to a terrible temptation to *exaggerate* the very excellent results that they did obtain so as utterly to confound their adversaries.

This type of exaggeration in reports is of course generally regarded in charitable circles as a venal sin. If, say the charitable workers, the only way to penetrate the stony-hearted treasuries of the world is to put forward reports that glow as much with imagination as with actual results—then, says the man in the field face to face with human misery, surely embroidery becomes a virtue? Anybody who is familiar with relief work will recognise this dilemma; if an absolutely exact account is given of the real work which is done in a tragic situation by any agency, many of the donors will find it insufficient, will become discouraged and will cease support. If, on the other hand, they are assured that for a minimum outlay they have not only rescued a refugee from danger of death, but fed him, given him an overcoat, found him a job, and educated his grandchildren at the university, they will probably go on contributing. For as one of my favourite characters in fiction said, " If you want to get men to act reasonably, you must set about persuading them in a maniacal manner." This is regrettable, but it is a fact which all organisations connected with charity—and politics—have to recognise.

But there is, of course, a nemesis. Exaggeration is a habit-forming drug, and after a time a considerable amount of doubt regarding the complete reality of the miraculous results grew up in the Assembly. It varied from the " provisional doubt " of the followers of Descartes to a Pyhronnic scepticism.

ii. *Reasons for the Omission.*

It is perhaps interesting to speculate for a moment on the possible *causes* of the omission in the Covenant of any specific reference to refugees.

It could hardly have been that those who catalogued the wrongs to be righted, that those who listed the dangers and impediments to the achievement of a braver new world, were ignorant of the existence and of the potential recrudescence of refugee problems.

The right of asylum is as old as human nature, and the tragedy of exile, the affliction of banishment, have always been one of the most striking misfortunes of history and, as such, are celebrated in play and poetry, in song and saga.

They occur frequently in Shakespeare's dramas. Did not Romeo refuse to be a refugee, and say to Friar Lawrence, when confronted with an expulsion order:

> " For exile hath more terror in his look,
> Much more than death . . . . . . "

and again,

> " . . . . . . Banishment!
> O friar, the damned use that word in hell;
> Howlings attend it . . . . . . "

History has known many refugee problems. There is nothing new under the sun. The Emperor Claudius, in A.D. 49, banished the Jews from Rome, and Aquila and his wife Priscilla were two of the refugees that resulted from his act, for we read in the Bible that they were evacuated—to use the modern term—to Corinth, where they met St. Paul.

Nor were the movements restricted to individual exiles. There were group movements and mass population exits. These mostly resulted from religious intolerance and from absolutism of one sort or another, theocratic, political, and nationalist. The flourishing German colonies in South Chile were due to the liberal revolution in Germany and many similar examples may be found all over the new world.

The great American nation itself was largely founded by refugees from religious and political intolerance, and that is perhaps why the citizens of the United States have always been so remarkably generous in their support of those who form an enormous and growing population. There is no doubt, may I say, in parenthesis, that the private effort which found expression in the work of the Near East Relief, the American Red Cross, and many other such organisations, was one of the most admirable features of the troubled decades which immediately followed the Armistice.

That being so, one cannot ascribe this omission to ignorance.

To what then was it due? Normally, when anything goes wrong in international work, when its failures seem to cry from the housetops, or when as in this case it seems that good results have fallen short of perfection, one is safe in putting the blame on the juridical conception of unlimited national sovereignty. This is not the place in which to give oneself the luxury of a full-throated criticism of the evil of unrestricted State sovereignty.

I should like, however, to baptise it as International Public Enemy No. 1, whilst, with the professional deformation that comes from long service with a tripartite and international organisation, remarking at the same time that most of those who criticise it appear to forget that, without it, most international organisations would lose their democratic character and tend inevitably to authoritarianism. Be that as it may, it is now, as Professor Mowat said in 1935,* "a thoroughly well-established concept, based on very powerful agencies."

It was perhaps, then, after all, fairly natural that an Assembly of sovereign States should have looked askance at any idea of including in an international instrument, anything which might by implication admit that State sovereignty could either become so unbearable that large masses of people would prefer destitution abroad to obeying its dictates at home, or that a State should find the tenets of its majorities so indigestible in the case of numerous minorities amongst its population, that it would be moved to expedite large masses of them over its frontiers in a manner the description of which compels meiosis in an international official. Let us charitably assume that such was the faith in the international new deal that was being propounded that it was considered that refugees could not be the permanent feature of the post-War world which they have unfortunately proved to be, and that therefore it was not considered necessary to tie the States

* *Problems of Peace,* Vol. X, p. 5.

to any obligations concerning them or to indicate clearly the provision of machinery to deal with them. It must also be remembered that previous to 1919 closed frontiers were a rarity and therefore refugee problems were nothing like so serious.

In spite of the constitutional difficulty, which I have referred to at such length because, in view of its repercussions, I consider it to be important, to the lasting credit of the League it must be recorded that for over 18 years it has tortured the texts, confounded the jurists, baffled the adepts of unrestricted sovereignty, and maintained what has been a very successful—in view of the difficulties—and quasi-permanent activity in favour of the refugees.

Through its various organs it played an important part in the solutions that were obtained in the problem of the resettlement of Greek refugees in Greece that resulted from the exchange of populations, an operation so greatly criticised at the time, but which has been one of the long-term successes of international organisation.

It considerably assisted the Bulgarian and Yugoslav Governments in their efforts to assimilate and assist masses of refugee population—and there are, perhaps, no Governments which have shown a more noble attitude than these. It was extremely active in the difficult problem of the Assyrians of Iraq, and its work for Russian refugees, refugees from the Saar, and refugees from Germany is known to all those who study the problem.

In order to give you some idea of the extent of refugee movements in the present-day world, may I add that the exhaustive list quoted above makes no mention of Italian refugees, Spanish refugees, Portuguese refugees, Chinese refugees or Abyssinian refugees.

iii. *What Assistance Has the League Actually Given to Refugees?*

What are the essential elements of international assistance to refugees? May I quote for a moment from the remarkable survey on the subject made by Sir John Hope-Simpson and his collaborators under the auspices of the Royal Institute of International Affairs. He says, when dealing with the problem of the future organisation of the refugee work and the moral and psychological value of League action, " One function that League control has fulfilled does not emerge from any description of organisation. The moral effect of the public assumption by the League of some responsibility for refugees, and the publicity given annually by discussions in the Assembly, cannot be quantitatively estimated. The League action has probably prevented some refugee movements or some denationalisation of political emigrants, because Governments have wished to avoid the embarrassment of the indirect criticism implied by public discussions of the fate of refugees from those Governments: it has probably prevented some Governments taking unduly harsh measures against refugees resident in their territory. Assembly resolutions may appear to be rather ineffective, because they have not sufficed to put an end to expulsions from countries of refuge, yet the restraint imposed by Governments' dislike of international publicity of domestic abuses has undoubtedly stopped or reduced much bureaucratic or merely thoughtless ill-treatment. "And," he adds, " in addition to these negative achievements, the mere existence of an international institution to protect refugees has been a standing recognition of an obligation on the conscience of the organised international world; it has assisted in the creation of an atmosphere facilitating the co-operation of the private and national organisations in international plans; and, above all, it has afforded great psychological benefit to the refugees themselves, by creating the belief that they are not entirely defenceless, that they have a supra-national guardian to whom they can ultimately appeal if they are, for instance, victimised by unjust police measures in the national territory in which they have sought asylum. Even if the appeal may not always lead to effective action, the possibility of making an appeal to a sympathetic office, official or commissioner is important in itself for refugees who feel acutely the isolation and the defencelessness of their position."

I do not wish to give the impression that the League action in the past has been of an entirely psychological nature. It has not. In spite of objections we have seen the whole gamut of action, ranging from the chartering of boats for evacuation, the provision of food and money for starving refugees, the organisation of assisted migration and colonisation, to the celebration of a network of conventions covering such questions as passports, juridical status, and the like—all these have been severely practical and concrete forms of assistance and it is right to add that if the League had not taken them up, much less would have been done for the refugees. In addition to the work of Nansen and his worthy successors, many other League organisations or committees have assisted in various ways—such, for example, as the Legal Section by its work on nationality, the Communications and Transit Organisation, the Committee of Experts on Indigent Foreigners, the Commission of Enquiry into the Traffic in Women and

Children in the Near East, the Health Organization, the Committee on Intellectual Co-operation and, last but not least, the International Labour Office, which not only co-operated with Dr. Nansen from 1921 to 1924, maintained the technical services on its Budget from 1925 to 1929, but still makes available its information and experience regarding problems of migration and colonisation.

iv. *How Should the Problem be Dealt With To-day?*

With the imprudence which I fear has always characterised those who are interested in refugees, I will now endeavour, with the greatest temerity, to rough out some ideas for obtaining more effective action through the mixed form of international machinery which seems to have been decided upon for one of the particular problems in the refuge field which is menacing the peace of the world and the happiness of hundreds of thousands of unfortunate persons at the present time. I refer to the pressing problem of Jewish and other refugees from Germany.

On the root cause of this problem I can hardly dwell here, for indeed there is much to be said in favour of what the Bishop of Gloucester wrote in a letter to the London *Times* a few days ago. Dealing with the duty of toleration and understanding the difficulties of both sides, he said, " There can be no peace without good-will. Would it not be wiser and more Christian if we were to attempt to show good will instead of indulging in a continuous and often unfair criticism which seems so often dictated by political animosity and is expressed in language which is neither diplomatic nor charitable? " There is a good deal in what the bishop says and we are always perhaps too ready to decry the scandals of other nations and turn a blind eye upon the defects of our own. If a refugee from Mars—that being, I suppose, the planet from which we should most likely receive an addition to our refugee problem—were to land upon this earth, he might find it hard to make a moral distinction between the existence of special non-Aryan benches in Berlin and Vienna and the existence of "Jim Crow" waiting rooms and railway wagons in the Southern States of America, or the difficulties which high caste Hindus find in obtaining accommodation in the more reasonably priced London hotels.

An international official can neither condemn nor condone. He should neither exacerbate political passion nor emasculate moral indignation. He can only explain, explore and expatiate, and follow the gentle precept of Spinoza, himself a Jew acquainted with the sorrows of his people, who, if he had been unlucky enough to live in this *civilised* era, would probably have been a refugee himself, when he suggested that we should *ne pas pleurer, ne pas s'indigner, mais comprendre,* in the knowledge that there is much to be said on both sides.

In order to *situate* the problem, however, the international official may be permitted to quote, nor need he confine himself to the calmer bishops. Unfortunately these problems are no new thing in history, which provides many examples of confusion, distress, disturbance and cruelty arising from racial and religious causes. Nor have such events been confined to the struggles of the Jews with other religions. There are many examples in Christian history itself of internecine struggles between those who held differing tenets of faith and differing ideas of what should be the conduct of those who hold such tenets when they have come into conflict with the requirements of sovereignty. In *King Henry VIII,* by William Shakespeare, there is a scene in which Bishop Gardiner reproaches Archbishop Cranmer with the result of his teaching of new beliefs and efforts at religious synchronisation.

> If we suffer—

(says the Bishop)

> Out of our easiness and childish pity
> To one man's honour, this contagious sickness,
> Farewell all physic: and what follows then?
> Commotions, uproars, with a general taint
> Of the whole State: as of late those our neighbours
> The upper Germany can dearly witness,
> Yet freshly pitied in our memories.

Mr. Myron Taylor, who is not a bishop but a late President of the United States Steel Corporation, is reported in *The Times* as having said, at the meeting of the Inter-Governmental Committee for Refugees which was set up by the Evian Conference, and which has recently met in London, that civilisation brings both a right and a duty. "The right is a sovereign right of each nation to promote the welfare of its citizens internally in the way of its choosing. The duty is the obligation imposed on each nation in promoting the welfare of its citizens not to trespass upon the rights of other nations."

M. Bérenger, of France, a country which has a noble record of refugee reception, put it this way: "The Government which expels the refugees should leave them their properties, which are up to the present their only means of livelihood. And the Governments who receive them should accord them the means of working, so that they may live. The hunting of a man, the appropriation of his property, the concentration camp, beyond which there is only the graveyard as a horizon—all that which is contrary to human dignity—can only result in a catastrophic disturbance of the relationship between nations."

I should like to add that it seems to me that M. Bérenger might include a third duty for nations which neither expel nor receive. It is to help those nations who, by a sort of geographical injustice, find themselves, as immediate neighbours to the expelling States, and on account of their recognition of the dictates of humanity, saddled with an unfair share of what should be a problem common to all civilisation.

The first conclusion is that there must be in any plan for palliation or relief of this problem as a pre-requisite, a better and more humane organisation of the exodus, and it is clear that, whilst those, who are applying the compulsion which is designed to produce departure, are unable to point to destinations to which the refugees can be regularly, legally and methodically despatched, the method of ensuring the desired movement is likely to be much more undesirable than if there existed definite reception centres. If it were in effect easier for the refugees to leave, the degree of compulsion would not be so great. What has proved such a shock to the world in this matter is not perhaps so much the decision that the refugees must go—though that decision caused the Colombian Delegate at Evian to request that a Committee should be set up to enquire into the international legality of mass denationalisation which resulted in quantities of human contraband being pushed over the frontiers—but the methods which have been used to bring about their departure.

On the other hand it is probably true that anything short of the measures actually taken would not have produced results. There is no doubt, for instance, that had possible countries been formally approached through the diplomatic channels and asked whether they would take large numbers of refugees from Germany in an orderly manner, they would certainly have said No. The proof of this is that, face to face not with a hypothetical but with an actual and tragic situation—(in the description of which the Pope was moved to quote Tacitus, and say: "We have no longer even the courage, the good sense, to give to things their name—'*vera etiam rerum perditimus nomina*'")—they have still declined in many instances, and left, as I have said, the burden to the immediate neighbours.

As for the extent of the problem—at the meeting of the London Committee, the following estimates were made: already 125,000 Jews, and tens of thousands of political refugees, have left Germany, mostly without money and many without papers; 15,000 Jews had, up to 3rd August, left Austria. Mr. Myron Taylor told the Committee that it must budget for an exodus of at least 600,000 from Germany in the next five years, including Jews, half-Jews and Roman Catholics. This, he said, meant the telescoping of sixteen years' normal emigration into five years. The U.S.A., he said, had already promised to take 27,370 during the present quota year, but at that rate the U.S.A. would have received 100,000 out of the 600,000 within five years. Now as to remedies.

The experts say in general terms (1) that the exodus must be made more methodical; (2) that other countries must do their share; and (3) that infiltration and naturalisation of refugees in the receiving countries is infinitely preferable to mass agricultural settlement or colonisation, because it appears that for any practical scheme settlement expenses may run as high as £1,000 per family. They propose to try and cover some of the finance required by the co-ordination of available charitable resources and Government assistance and the establishment of revolving funds such as that set up by Dr. Nansen for his own refugee settlement work. There is also general agreement that it is really necessary for the German Government to allow the refugees to take at least some of their property with them, so that they shall not start completely destitute in any country for which they can manage to obtain a visa.

v. *Reluctance of Countries to Admit Refugees.*

It is now necessary to take a "realistic" attitude and examine for a moment the reasons why countries, even when they are compelled by world public opinion and their own liberal constitutions to agree in principle and in public to accept certain categories of refugees, very often in fact do not implement their agreement by allowing their consulates to issue visas, but in fact produce opposite instructions of a confidential nature which effectively prevent either visas or *permis de séjour* being issued. Everybody who is familiar with the problem of immigration knows of this situation. The acceptance in principle is so hedged about with financial conditions which most refugees cannot fulfil, with requirements of what may be described as certificates of correct ideology and the possession of agricultural qualifications and so on, that in practice the process of what is called somewhat euphemistically "infiltration" really would better be described as stagnation and starvation. And this I fear will always be so unless something is done to remove the reasons—the very valid reasons upon which this attitude is based.

If anybody believes that I have over-stated this apparent discrepancy between theoretical opportunities of migration and the actual impossibility of going anywhere, I should like to refer them to a letter which appeared from a refugee in the *Manchester Guardian* and from which I will read you the following extract:

> " . . . . . . I gather from your letter that you also—in common with everybody abroad without any exception—have absolutely no conception of the frightful, nerve-shattering difficulties one is faced with in the matter of immigration. Until recently Colombia was in fact virtually the only country which permitted entry. Now this has changed, and I am afraid that I shall never be able to get in there now. I think it may interest you to have the collected facts about the immigration difficulties. Here they are: United States.—Affidavit. Quota. Pedantic bureaucracy. At the earliest it requires three months from the day when the affidavit is received, if this is considered satisfactory by the Consulate, before emigration is possible. Britain.—In the most favourable circumstances, and with influence, visa only without working permit (except in the case of domestic service). Everything must be done from the English side. Even then endless delay through the Consulate. France, Belgium, Holland, Switzerland.—Completely closed. Even heavily restricted transit visas very difficult to obtain. Italy.—No visa. Autonomous frontier officers, who send Jews back from the frontier. Transit visas possible. Czechoslovakia, Hungary, the Balkans.—Hermetically sealed."
> And so the melancholy list goes on.
>
> May I add that since the Evian Conference five countries have produced public laws or decrees covering more stringent conditions for entry.

I should not like it to be thought that I consider such an attitude invariably unreasonable. If one places oneself for a moment in the position of the receiving country, with its eagerness to preserve a coherent nationalism, with its own unemployment problem, with its own ideological conflict, either open or latent, with its organised workers fearful of the lowering influence on wages of the admission of destitutes, with its professional men firmly resisting any unauthorised entry into their closely guarded and overcrowded ranks, there is no doubt that very often the instructions sent really do correspond more to the will of the people than the comfortable words of the Delegates at Conferences, for human nature is only capable of limited self-sacrifice and it soon becomes insensible to misery with which it does not come into immediate contact. Furthermore, there are so many national problems and at the moment *such* a superabundance of international tragedies that a certain lessening of international sympathy is not surprising.

This point was well put 17 years ago by one of Mr. Aldous Huxley's characters in one of his earlier novels, who goes on record with the following devastating statement which remains as true to-day as it was then : " Mr. Scogan drank off what was left of his port and refilled the glass. 'At this very moment,' he went on, 'the most frightful horrors are taking place in every corner of the world. People are being crushed, slashed, disembowelled, mangled; their dead bodies rot and their eyes decay with the rest. Screams of pain and fear go pulsing through the air at the rate of 1,100 feet per second. After travelling three seconds they are perfectly inaudible. These are distressing facts.' " Mr. Scogan concludes his remarks by saying that a really sympathetic race would not so much as know the meaning of happiness.

These migration restrictions exist, furthermore, not only in the case of refugees, but in the case of more ordinary or non-denationalised migrants who wish to migrate for purely economic reasons, and who may still count upon the protection of their Governments, but—and this is important—they are immeasurably increased in the case of refugees, because of the irrevocable nature of refugee migration.

Economists and demographic experts argue continually as to the effect of increases and decreases of population upon unemployment and the economic situation generally. Roughly speaking, the optimists say "the more the merrier," whilst the pessimists take an entirely opposite view. Although I am neither an economist, nor an optimist nor a pessimist, I am inclined to consider that Mr. Douglas Jay, the City Editor of the *Daily Herald,* was not far off a measure of truth when he said "ultimately a nation is almost bound to be richer if the productive power of a large additional number of persons is added to its own. In so far as refugees consume, they are helping to increase population; in so far as they produce, they are adding to the national income." There is, of course, a good deal of "ultimately" and "in so far as" in this cautious pronouncement, but history has provided a good many examples of its truth and I think one might accept it in that form, though I fear it is unlikely to impress any consul to the point of awarding a visa about which he would otherwise be doubtful.

The real difficulty about receiving a refugee is that if he turns out badly, becomes a charge upon public funds, goes in for subversive activities, lowers the standard of living—and all these things have been known to happen—there is no way of getting rid of him. It is no use putting him over the frontier in the middle of the night. He will inevitably be returned. There are many cases of unfortunate refugees who pass long periods of their lives in prison. Having illegally entered one country, they are expelled into another. The second country refuses to accept them, and returns them, whereupon they are placed in prison for having effected illegal entry. This is an endemic situation in refugee affairs, and no palliative will be efficacious unless it deals with this impasse. It is comparatively easy to get States to agree to issue a Nansen or other passport to Stateless persons, but it is very difficult to get a visa, valid for entry, upon that passport, and it is doubly difficult to get the State which issues the passport to agree to receive the refugee back into its territory as if he were a national, should the necessity arise. That is why every consulate everywhere thinks twice and three times before accepting a refugee finally, and that is why it is so difficult for them to move in search of employment. That is also why the remedy of infiltration is slow, tragic, beset by temptations to illegality and by starvation. There is no doubt that if the irrevocable aspects of reception of refugees could be diminished, if it could be made possible to send them off to try again somewhere else if they did not fit, the question of finding employment and future settlement and naturalisation would be greatly eased. This being the key of the problem, it seems that in the first place efforts must be concentrated on finding some remedy.

I should add that a further very considerable obstacle

exists and it is that which lies in the difficulty when refugees have been temporarily admitted to a country, of keeping track of them and of seeing that they do not exceed the temporary *permis de séjour* which has been given them. This again makes them a considerable nuisance to the authorities and militates against even their temporary reception, and our remedy should endeavour to diminish this objection also.

It is, I fear, quite clear that by means of "infiltration" and mass settlement, in view of these and other difficulties, nothing like the numbers that require to be moved will be able to depart in an orderly manner in the near future unless something of a rather special nature is done, and it is obviously necessary from a humanitarian point of view not to keep thousands of people living in fear, depression and misery with a veritable Sword of Damocles hanging over them for a moment longer than can possibly be helped. For it is unfortunately a fact and has been through the ages, that cruelty breeds cruelty and intolerance and oppression produce long-term reprisals. Similarly the exaggeration of certain racial characteristics, over-concentration on business, commercial, financial, artistic and professional pursuits to the neglect of agricultural, labouring and artisan occupations, the financial exploitation of the simple, the avoidance of complete identification with the country of residence together with the practice of a racial solidarity which, though it may be admirable, is bound to be an object of suspicion to the ordinary national, and a faculty for the *reductio ad absurdum* of certain weaknesses of the capitalist and democratic systems: these defects, originally no doubt the products of cruelty and oppression, have continued for hundreds of years to engender reactions and explosions of a quite unwarranted intensity which in their turn have only had the effect of increasing the characteristics complained of. And so the vicious circle goes on. And it is the duty of civilisation to put a stop to it and as quickly as possible to prevent the intensification which is going on to-day. For as I say the Nemesis of cruelty is more cruelty, of unreason more unreason.

One of the reasons for the success of the exchange of populations between Greece and Turkey was that it was done comparatively quickly in an orderly manner, under the control of League Commissions, and that as the numbers were so large, organisation was inevitably imposed. If it had been left to " infiltration " the situation would have been impossibly tragic. Not that I wish to stop infiltration when it can be effected without undue hardship. For a small percentage it will always continue to be the best method and there is no doubt also that in the phase of *settlement* it is a superior method. What I wish to point out is that in the phase of exodus it is subject to the grave defects which I have endeavoured to describe.

vi. *The First Step Towards Settlement—" Transitional Centres."*

The remedy—or perhaps I had better say the palliative—that I would propose is this. In my experience, in order to obtain attention, funds for relief and proper measures generally in any refugee problem, it is necessary to pursue a centripetal policy during the phase of exodus.

In other words, in order to assist refugees, provide an immediate destination and consequently an orderly exit, a policy of establishing transitional centres in the countries of refuge, and not in the countries of origin, must be adopted.

In dealing with such problems as feeding, housing and doctoring, it is much easier to run a camp or similar organisation than it is to perform the same services for persons who are endeavouring to " infiltrate " and are scattered all over the bordering countries of the expelling State, often without proper papers or *permis de séjour.*

I would therefore advocate the immediate establishment of a considerable number of such transitional centres or zones in as many countries as possible, but—and this is the important innovation—when refugees had entered these transitional centres they would not be regarded as having legally entered the country in which the centre was established or as having acquired *ipso facto* and immediately the right to move freely in that country or to take up employment in it.

It is not, of course, proposed to " confine the refugees to barracks " indefinitely, for in the settlement phase of the operation the centripetal trend or policy of concentration has to be gradually but firmly reversed and a centrifugal policy or policy of dispersal must take its place. It is then that infiltration may be stimulated and larger group movements providing for overseas colonisation may be encouraged.

Visas to leave the transitional camps or centres would be given after examination of individual cases and for longer or shorter periods as seemed requisite. If a reasonably permanent *modus vivendi* appears to have been achieved by any refugee or group of refugees, a semi-permanent *permis de séjour* might be granted on leaving the camp, the first formalities of naturalisation might begin and new refugees might be received from the country of expulsion to replace those who have left. If, on the other hand, a refugee became destitute shortly after leaving the centre, he would have to return to it again. But, in this case, he would not be the insoluble problem that he is now; the police and other authorities, knowing of the existence of the centre, would have a humane solution available and the refugee, knowing that such a solution existed, would not be tempted to avoid control or adopt illegal measures to enable him to stay where he was.

Similarly, potential employers who can hardly be expected to contemplate the responsibility and general difficulty of offering employment to an unknown person in Germany or of giving the very binding guarantees which are usually—and rightly—demanded by the authorities in the country of reception, would have the opportunity of offering experimental employment to persons whom they could interview personally without incurring any responsibility at all, for they would know that if things did not turn out well the refugees they employed would go back to their centres.

I have no doubt that this would greatly increase the available volume of refugee employment.

As a great deal of the employment potentially available for refugees is liable to be of a seasonal nature, it is also obvious that it would be much easier to produce a supply for this demand from centres such as I have described than in any other way.

As for the organisation of overseas migration and colonisation or of migration from one country to another, there would again be a distinct advantage, for it would be possible to guarantee to the receiving country that at any time, if a real necessity arose, the refugee migrants could be returned to the transition centre from which they had come, thereby avoiding the "irrevocable" visa difficulty which has already been referred to.

Such a measure, which could be combined with a system of insurance covering the payment of a small premium in respect of all the members of the migrant group in order to provide for the cost of return to the centre of any eventually unsuitable member, would enormously facilitate possibilities of migration, for it would not only relieve the authorities of the receiving country of their preoccupation about what would happen if the scheme failed and the migrants did not find suitable employment and began to drift to already over-populated centres, but would have a favourable reaction on the attitude of the refugee migrant himself who, knowing that if the worst came to the worst he could always come back, would be more ready to contemplate the adventure of colonisation and would enter upon it in a more courageous state of mind.

There are, however, certain other advantages. These transitional centres would also greatly facilitate the organisation of training and rehabilitation. It would be possible to organise them with their own hospitals and medical relief system and this method of organisation would certainly be more efficient and would therefore cost less than the provision of sporadic relief to refugees scattered in a great many different places. As far as rationing and similar types of assistance are concerned, the same advantage would be gained. From the point of view of finance and charitable appeal, it would certainly be easier to obtain money from private, semi-official and official sources if a large and tangible scheme of this sort was in existence, for publicity would be easier and donors would have proper guarantees and would know that there would be something to show for their money. Such a charitable concentration, enabling everybody to give to a practical plan sponsored by Governments in which overlapping had been avoided, would certainly facilitate the collection of the necessary funds.

There is no time to go deeply into the practical régime under which these camps would be run, nor to indicate where they could be best established. It is obvious that there would have to be international co-operation and that the details would have to be settled at a properly prepared Conference. It is also equally clear that the Jewish organisations would have to take a large measure of responsibility for the establishment, upkeep and maintenance of the centres and that they would be required to collaborate with the national authorities so as to obtain the maximum of assurances that the centres would be properly maintained and that guarantees given in the cases of individual refugees allowed to depart from them would be properly implemented.

It is also possible that in the not unlikely event of other refugee problems suddenly descending upon this unhappy world, adaptations of this plan for them would prevent a great deal of human misery. Therefore, it would appear to be desirable that the international machinery, which I suggest should study this plan, should bear this possibility in mind when elaborating its details.

In so far as concerns that machinery and the international aspects of the plan, it seems to me that agreement would have to be made internationally covering the general regime of the centres, their location, their capacity and for the organisation of visa facilities for the centrifugal phase based on the guarantees that I have described. In the field of finance also it would appear advisable to devise methods, for equalising the expenditure on these centres so as to arrive at a reasonably equitable division, for the organisation of international loans and Revolving Funds, and for the best methods of obtaining financial assistance from countries where exchange restrictions are in force.

The final and most practical advantage would seem to me to be that if such a plan were set up it would be possible to make a friendly and constructive approach to the German Government and to point out that the possibility of introducing some measure of order and respectability into this movement of population, for it is nothing less, was really dependent on the adoption of the plan and that this in turn depended upon German collaboration.

At the present moment, owing to the absence of even a faintly plausible plan, there seems to be no practical basis of negotiation with the German Government except the formation of a Committee and the formulation of reproach. The orderly solution of this problem would do a great deal to improve the fevered atmosphere of the world as it is at the moment. Confidence—particularly in the democracies—in the ultimate sanity of the human race is so terribly shaken that if things are allowed to go on as they are at present without the intervention of practical and ordered remedies for those aberrations of human conduct which *are* susceptible of peaceful solution, it will become even further weakened and further degeneration will set in with results that no man can foresee.

On the other hand, a determination to control the situation by appropriate action and not only to talk about it would so greatly restore confidence as to make the cost an investment for civilisation which would pay for itself a thousand times over.

CHAPTER XII

FOR WHAT SHOULD NATIONAL POWER BE USED?

by

W. ARNOLD-FORSTER

TEN years ago, when first I had the honour of addressing the Geneva Institute of International Relations, the League was thriving and Geneva was the political centre of the world. When I spoke five years ago the League's cause was in danger, and I remember saying, as a thunderstorm crashed outside, that one could almost hear the foundations of civilisation cracking outside beyond these walls of glass.* And now, on this still night in 1938, what can you hear with the ear of imagination? Bombs falling on Canton, on Valencia: screams of those dying now in wars involving some six hundred million people in Asia, in Europe—yes, and in Africa too: moans of men beaten in concentration camps: the hammering of the armourers in the greatest armament race ever known. To-day, Geneva has become a backwater. To-day, some of you may be asking yourselves whether this may not prove to be the last paper in the series called "Problems of Peace."

In such a situation, I have been given the task of reviewing the fundamental problem of choice of direction in foreign policy, and of suggesting the outlines of a con-

* Mr. Arnold-Forster's paper five years ago was read in the "glass room" of the Palais Wilson, then used as the League's Council Chamber.—Ed.

structive peace policy. Could any task be more difficult? How glad I should be if, ten years hence, I could read this paper without finding that the words used were either too optimistic or too defeatist, too confident or too lacking in resolution.

I propose to see first whether we can agree upon a long-range objective in international policy. Then I will suggest some short-range objectives, compatible with this long-range aim and appropriate to the moral and material power available. Lastly, I will venture a few suggestions as to what we might do as individuals.

i. *Our Long-range Objective. Commonwealth or Tribalism?*

Firstly, do you agree that, fundamentally, *the world is one place?* Do you agree that the human race must learn to live as a commonwealth, not merely as a collection of contending tribes? Do you believe that the power and energy of all the diverse elements of this commonwealth can and must be liberated from the obsessions that now result from the tribal war system? Do you believe that, for this positive creative purpose, we must evolve a system of world government competent to suppress war and to contribute effectively to the solution of all those problems which properly become the concern of the commonwealth? Do you agree that, on the road towards this universal commonwealth, we need a Society of Nations, not necessarily universal at this stage, whose members do sincerely accept certain elementary standards of peaceful behaviour, with all that this implies? Do you agree, too, with Mr. Carritt, that such a commonwealth cannot be surely founded except on a basis of free and informed public opinion? Do you agree with Mr. Rothstein and other speakers that it will involve far-reaching changes in the social and economic basis of capitalist society, including an extensive subordination of the private profit motive: and that in particular the form of exploitation which is included under the label Imperialism must be got rid of? Do you agree too that we may properly expect that, with the growth of the sense of commonwealth, there will be a growing sense that certain standards of toleration, justice and mercy are not simply a matter of concern to the individual tribes, but are properly a matter concerning the whole society? In short, do you share that creed which has been emerging, year after year, in the contributions of the diverse speakers before this Institute? Do you take sides in the great "ideological conflict" between those who believe in commonwealth and those who believe in tribalism?

Do not suppose that that is just a rhetorical question. It is fundamental, dividing the world. And let us not be misled by the claim that all peoples and all rulers really desire such a commonwealth, with all that it implies in renunciation of the war method. And let us not assume that Mussolini and Hitler and the Japanese militarists are the only rulers who are in effect on the side of tribalism to-day. For my part, I believe that Mr. Chamberlain's government, whilst desiring "peace at almost any price" as sincerely as any of its critics, is actually using British national power and influence rather as a tribal instrument for the service of self-judged "honour and vital interests" than as a contribution to the collective power which should be available for protection of what the Covenant calls "the peace of nations." Mr. Cordell Hull goes on steadfastly educating his country by beautiful speeches about the evil and futility of the policy of " Am I my brother's keeper " : but the actual policy of his Government in the most important issues is almost entirely self-regarding, tribal, except within the range of the now extended Monroe doctrine. A conspicuous example is the undiscriminating embargo policy embodied in the present Neutrality Law—a policy which is still defended by a section of the American peace movement. I hope American friends present will forgive my candidly expressing the opinion that so long as that law remains in its present form, the United States will be contributing to the growth of autarchy, and will not only be repudiating for herself the responsibility of sharing effectively in collective action to prevent aggression but will be actually strengthening the hands of the tribalists everywhere.

I will assume, however, that everyone here accepts such a commonwealth as I have indicated as a proper long-range objective of international policy, and desires that his own country should be quick to accept and promote the necessary curtailments of national sovereignty.

ii. *Short-range Objectives.*

What, then, are some of the short-range objectives that we should be aiming at, in present circumstances, or in such conditions as we can reasonably hope to create, given resolute democratic leadership?

Suppose that you were Foreign Secretary, and that the long-range aim of your policy was the building up of a peacefully-ordered, comprehensive commonwealth. You would have to choose day by day between policies tending towards tribalism, or policies tending towards world-government; you would either try to "make anarchy work" with the minimum of injury from competitive alliances and armaments, or else you would try patiently to create conditions in which a collective peace system could work properly. And in either case your choice of policy would be governed by the amount of power, material and moral, which you could hope to mobilise in support of that policy, at the right time and in the right place. (I assert this without attempting to discuss it; for I maintain that the real choice before a Foreign Secretary is not between power and no power, but between power enlisted behind some common code of peaceful behaviour, or power used outside of "law," simply as an instrument of national policy.)

ii. (A) *Making Anarchy Work?*

The policies now being pursued by Governments almost everywhere appear to be based on the despairing hope of "making anarchy work." Not a single Government, except perhaps in Russia, Spain and New Zealand, seems to be making an effort to build up an effective common front against war. Many excellent sermons have been preached, and some practical attempts are being made, with a view to the lowering of trade barriers and the promotion of a more acceptable, more prosperous peace: but these attempts remain without substantial effect, largely owing to the failure to master the war system with all its poisonous consequences. The economic palliatives proposed in the Van Zeeland Report, for instance, are blocked by political obstacles.

I see virtually no signs of effort to restore the shattered credit of the League. Mr. Chamberlain, in his speech of February 22nd, 1938, went so far as to tell the League's members in effect that each must fend for himself: *Sauve qui peut.* And that is what they are doing now, retreating from the collective defence of a common covenant of peace, scrambling instead for a kind of "security" which is impossible of attainment. Within a few weeks we may even see the British Government taking the lead at the coming Assembly in formulating some Resolution declaring that the sanctions of the Covenant, economic as well as military, must be regarded henceforth as not obligatory under any conditions but purely "optional."

Meanwhile, the attempt to make anarchy work is being pursued with vigour and astonishing optimism.

(1) *Spain and the Anglo-Italian Agreement.* Look, for instance, at the Anglo-Italian Agreement. When Mr. Eden resigned, he warned his countrymen that negotiations with Italy for such an agreement, undertaken in the circumstances of that time, were likely to injure rather than strengthen the foundations upon which international confidence must rest. Already the sequel shows, I think, that his prediction was right. You cannot restore confidence in the League whilst offering to the League's declared opponent an imperialist deal at the League's expense. You cannot even hope to weaken a Rome-Berlin axis by promoting the triumph of the Rome-Berlin policy in Spain, and by agreeing, as part of a bilateral bargain, to flout the League and recognise the King of Italy as lawful ruler of the whole of an Ethiopia still largely unconquered. The Anglo-Italian Agreement (which may never come into force) apparently permits Mussolini to retain in Spain until the Spanish War is over

all the war material which he has sent there and which is what Franco chiefly needs. Indeed, the Agreement is, in effect, conditional upon Franco's victory against progressive Spain—a victory which, as previous speakers have emphasised, is actually desired by some people, some classes, in England, France and America. The British Government, thus influenced, and deeply anxious, of course, lest the war should become more extended, is content to shut its eyes to the continued reinforcements from Italy to Franco without which the Italian forces could not possibly be sustaining the huge effort of which the Fascist Press boasts every week. The British Government even puts pressure upon the French Government and on British shipowners to complete Franco's cordon around governmental Spain, without awaiting reciprocal action by Franco's foreign allies. This policy is not, never has been, never will be, real "non-intervention": nor does it accord in any respect with the principles of the Covenant: it amounts to a form of connivance at the victory of Fascism in Spain, a victory which would involve Italian and German control of crucial strategic positions both in the Mediterranean and on the Atlantic trade routes. I do not pretend to understand how British official strategists, concerned about protection of British shipping, can have the slightest confidence in this policy. I can only suppose that a policy in Spain which must tend to paralyse France must enormously increase the risks inherent in the present British policy towards France and Czechoslovakia. The physical increase of British armament is being discounted by a far-reaching strategic disarmament.

(2) *Ethiopia.* When I turn to the tragic story of the betrayal of Ethiopia, here too I find a disarmament of

Britain—in this case a moral disarmament. Lord Halifax made himself virtually the agent of Mussolini's policy of humiliating the League, by declaring that Britain would recognise the Italian conquest as lawful. Surely it was not honourable to sell that recognition as a bargain; nor would it be lawful to do so bilaterally, in disregard of the League's authoritative resolution interpreting the Covenant. It is not in accordance with the facts, since Ethiopia is far less effectively conquered and controlled by Italy than ever Belgium was by Germany after the end of 1914. And I cannot think that it is even an astute move in the moment's game of power politics, especially on the part of a country which has need of the sympathy of American public opinion, or on the part of an Empire whose 470 million inhabitants include only 70 million whites.

(3) *China.* When we turn to the Far East, here again we find that the game of power politics is being played with what seems a strange recklessness. There are three policies which might be followed:

(*a*) We might adopt a policy of cautious, isolated, withdrawal from any attempt to protect any interests, national or international, anywhere in that world east of Singapore over which the Japanese militarists are flinging out their vast ambitions. Discreetly evacuate Hong Kong, which has become a hostage, not an asset. Abandon Hainan and Indo-China and the defence of the Philippines. Withdraw foreign warships from the Yangtse, drop the attempt to protect foreign lives and property by means of menaces and protests to Japan, and drastically recast and curtail our naval armament programmes. There is something to be said for such a policy.

(*b*) Or we might try to secure cautious but effective

collective action to restrain Japanese aggression by prohibiting the import of Japanese goods and by stopping our exports of war material, including oil, to Japan. This policy, to be effective, would need the collaboration of the British Commonwealth, the United States, Russia, France and Holland. It might, improbably, lead to naval reprisals by Japan; precautionary measures for defence of the East Indian oil-fields would be called for, and it might be necessary to face the (temporary) loss of control in Hong Kong and elsewhere. There is much to be said for such a policy.

(*c*) The third possible policy—the one which is actually being followed—is one of isolated challenge to Japan. Admiral Yarnell up the Yangtse river, and Lord Halifax in the House of Lords, have recently used the language of menace towards Japan, warning her that the power of the United States, the power of Britain, might be used for the protection of their national interests. Each Government is acting alone, not for a cause greater than Britain's or America's, a cause which is China's and the League's, but simply for the commercial interests of their own nationals. Each Government backs its protests by displaying a small naval force within the jaws of the powerful Japanese mouse-trap. Each Government has tried the same policy again and again during recent years, without succeeding in preserving the interests they sought to safeguard. Surely, this policy is, of all the possible policies, the most certainly dangerous and the least likely to prove effective. Politically, it is futile, even disastrous. Morally, it is atrocious.

Consider the moral aspect. In February, 1933, and again in October, 1937, our Governments joined in condemning Japan's aggression, declaring it to be a violation of various treaties made with us. The Mayors of very many of the chief cities of the democratic countries have lately joined in the public protest against the ruthless Japanese bombing of open cities in China, and the massacre of civilians. Yet the very cities which these mayors preside over are continuing, month after month, to make blood-money out of supplying the Japanese with indispensable oil and metals and aeroplanes and purchasing power. The British Empire and the United States have between them, as Mr. Stimson has pointed out, the means of preventing the success of Japan's aggression, if only they will devise the "simple means of international co-operation which would stop our participation in this slaughter." Yet the participation continues. Such hypocrisy exposes us to the scorn of the Japanese. Such betrayal exposes us to the enduring resentment of the Chinese. Is it not revolting to ourselves and to those whose help or sympathy Britain may need in a day of trouble?

Look at the policy from a political and economic standpoint. Can it really serve our national interests in the long run? Has it not led to disaster enough already (*e.g.* in encouraging Italy's Ethiopian adventure?) And is it not leading even now to further disasters, for the Eastern peoples and for ourselves? It must tend to keep Japan fettered by a triumphant military caste; and it must tend to thwart and pervert the resurgent genius of the Chinese continent. Is that what the democratic peoples really desire? And it must serve to smash the moral and material foundations of our own defence against aggression in the West as well as in the East. If it be granted that the " interests " we are properly concerned to defend include above all those principles of peace-keeping which were accepted in our Covenant and Kellogg Pact and Nine Power Treaty, then we injure ourselves in dishonouring our obligations towards the Chinese, whose struggle is our struggle also. To arm the enemies of what the Covenant calls " the peace of nations," whilst withholding even financial aid from its defenders, is not " realism " but self-destruction. Even if we were only concerned to defend the commercial interests of our fellow-nationals in the Far East, the present policy would be a ruinous one : it is not prudent for British imperialists who cling to the Ottawa policy of imperial protection to facilitate Japan's economic subjugation of China, in the hope that a Japanese conqueor will accord equality of opportunity to British traders.

But, it may be argued, the betrayal of China and the avoidance of any action which might provoke the Japanese militarists, is now, and was in 1931-33, unavoidable : it was a painful necessity imposed upon us by compelling military and political circumstances. In 1932 the Singapore base was not ready, and neither the Russians nor the Americans were in the League. In 1937 we had our anxieties in the Mediterranean and elsewhere, near home. After the growth of American distrust of the British Government's policy, and after the unfavourable response of American opinion to President Roosevelt's Chicago speech of October, 1937, the difficulties of enlisting sure American support for collective economic pressure on Japan, with its attendant risks, have undoubtedly become formidable. But was a resolute attempt ever made to secure such collective action? I doubt it. Indeed, I venture to doubt whether Sir John Simon ever wanted such action to be taken, or believed that it would really be desirable to prevent Japan's "expansion" by conquest in Asia.

At the time of the Manchurian invasion, there were admittedly great risks and difficulties in the way of effective collective action "to protect the covenants of the League." To-day, in the invasion of China proper, the risks and difficulties of *isolated* action, to protect purely British or American interests, must be more grave, not less. No layman, being without access to the Government's information, can have fully adequate material for judgment in such a matter: but I must express the opinion for what it is worth that the League's Members and the United States, in adopting a policy of "am I my brother's keeper" towards China, have chosen the greater rather than the lesser risk.

(4) *British Disarmament.* Mr. Chamberlain has lately declared that Britain has "interests in China and that we cannot stand by and see them sacrificed": and this concern for British interests, natural enough in itself, appears to be the only basis for British action in the matter. Mr. Chamberlain says further (July 26th, 1938) that no one "should imagine for one moment that, although we seek peace, we are willing to sacrifice, even for peace, British honour and British vital interests." Slipping easily back, you see, into the language of international anarchy, back to that same dishonoured slogan by which each contending tribe sought to justify its "sacred egoism" in the days before the Covenant was born. Mr. Chamberlain has said too (February 22nd, 1938) that in his view "the League will never do its best work" so long as its

members are bound "to use force in support of obligations"—*i.e.,* obligations to share in the protection of a common rule of peace-keeping. Well, the actual alternative to such pooling of power for a social purpose is not the disuse of national power but its anarchic use in support of conflicting "national interests," so-called "honour and vital interests." If we return this answer to the question, "For what should national power be used?" then we throw the collective peace system overboard: and incidentally we destroy any hope of putting a stop to the armaments race. I believe this is the road to war. It is also the quick road to the liquidation of those forces, moral as well as material, which Britain would need to have on her side in the event of war. If the British abandon the principle of the Covenant, they abandon "imponderables" which, as Napoleon knew, are not less important than the armaments in the national arsenals. They divide Britain itself, divide the Dominions, alienate American opinion, and liquidate the potentially powerful association of League Members against aggression.

British opinion is, I believe, more profoundly divided now upon foreign policy than ever in my life-time before (unless in regard to Czechoslovakia). It is no accident that you see now a former Conservative First Lord of the Admiralty, Mr. Churchill, and a former Labour First Lord, Mr. Alexander, both advocating a policy of "Back to the Covenant" as affording the only basis upon which the needed national unity can be secured.

In the Dominions, too, the British move away from the Covenant and the discrediting of the League, have had a divisive effect. In Canada, for instance, there is now a quickened anxiety about the risks of being entangled in the consequences of a policy in London which is widely regarded as having become purely opportunist and unpredictable. There is always a latent division between those Canadians who emphasise Canada's British connections, and those who emphasise her essential North-Americanism. That division can remain unimportant so long as Britain's foreign policy and Canada's are both following lines—railway lines, so to speak—laid down in common covenants of peace. But the moment that the government in London runs off the lines of the Covenant, on to a policy which is essentially self-regarding, anarchic, then Canada becomes a divided nation and the Canadian government moves towards isolation. To-day Mr. Mackenzie King is sitting painfully on the fence, having accepted, of course, no obligation to participate in the defence of British interests, and having virtually repudiated on Canada's behalf any obligation to participate in sanctions, whether military or economic, in any case whatever.

As for New Zealand, I need not remind you of her Government's reaction towards the betrayal of Ethiopia. And as for India, we should not forget the extremely significant warning by Congress last Spring that the Indian people simply would not fight with Britain in a war for British honour and vital interests.

As for the United States, the present trend of policy here, especially in England, is having the effect of alienating public opinion. I had opportunities of seeing something of the unfavourable reaction of American opinion at the time of the Manchurian disaster (when Sir John Simon declared that " however this matter is handled, I mean to see to it that my country does not get into trouble "). I also saw something of the strong reaction after the Hoare-

Laval plan and the betrayal of Ethiopia. And lately I have been seeing the still more unfavourable reaction after the resignation of Mr. Eden, the Anglo-Italian Agreement, and the British Government's recent treatment of governmental Spain. I gained the impression that there has been, during the past fifteen months, a widespread movement of opinion away from the non-moral attitude towards war which was expressed in the undiscriminating embargo policy of the Neutrality Law: and I expect that movement will grow, with powerful help from women's organisations such as the League of Women Voters. But I was deeply impressed also by the indications I found everywhere I went of distrust and anxiety about the present policy of the British Government. It may be fair to say—I think it is—that the average American who criticises the Chamberlain policy does not sufficiently appreciate how serious are the risks (avoidable or unavoidable) which the British Government has now to assess in any choice of policy. It may be fair for an Englishman to ask the American, "What ground have you for urging the British to accept any great risks for the defence of world peace if you do not urge your own country to accept a much lesser share of risk." But I am only concerned now to record the observed fact that the Chamberlain policy does seem, whether justifiably or not, to have alienated American opinion to a remarkable extent: so much so that for the present any latent swing of opinion away from isolationism seems likely to be without substantial political result, unless some great crisis arises.

As for the effect of recent events upon the League as a whole, and especially on the smaller European States,

I need only refer to the review of " the flight from collective security "—may I say, the frank and courageous review—given by Senator Rolin. The policy of the British and French governments in the Ethiopian ordeal, and in Spain and China, and such speeches as Mr. Chamberlain's on February 22nd, 1938, have slashed the bonds of loyalty which were beginning to tie the League together as a protection against aggression. The governments have weakened the foundations on which international confidence must rest, and in doing so have weakened their own defences. If a " realistic " policy is one which is justified by its fruits, the recent attempt to " make anarchy work " has not deserved the name of " realism."

ii. (B) *Making a Collective Peace System Work?*

I turn then to the alternative policy of trying to create conditions in which a collective peace system could be built up—or rebuilt—and made to work properly.

What is the collective peace system? What arguments are used against it? What can be done to make it practicable?

(1) *What is the Collective Peace System?* I need not here define in any detail what that omnibus phrase, " collective peace system," covers. But I may mention that when speaking at this Institute three years ago,* I did summarise seven essential elements of such a system, namely, *regular conference,* with certain elementary *rules* of pacific behaviour; constructive *services of peace;* provision for *peaceful settlement* of international disputes; provision for *peaceful change* of existing rights; *general*

* See *Problems of Peace,* 10th series (Allen & Unwin): or, for a fuller discussion, *The Intelligent Man's Way to Prevent War* (Gollancz), Chapters V and VI.

disarmament; and *collective action to prevent war,* or (failing prevention) *to stop it* with the minimum of injury to civilisation. I held that League Members are properly charged with the duty of co-operating in whatever measures are possible and effective to prevent aggression and to stop it. I emphasised that, contrary to the view held by a section of the peace movement in Britain and America, positive action to make the peace acceptable and fruitful, and negative action to prevent and stop aggression, are not alternative but complementary. And I maintained that the authors of the Covenant were compelled to steer cautiously between demanding too much and too little surrender of national sovereignty by members of the League : that the curtailment of sovereignty implicit in loyal League membership is more considerable than is commonly recognised by the League's impatient critics; and that it is no good insisting that nothing can be done about collective security or general disarmament or peaceful change until an all-round surrender of sovereignty, so complete as to revolutionise world-politics, has been achieved. Of course, there may be both need and opportunity now for some big further curtailment of sovereignty, some substantial new step towards making defence against aggression the function of a federal authority. But the general advance can, I am convinced, only be piecemeal, step by step; the new loyalties necessary to sustain a working system of "world government" cannot be expected to become strong bonds overnight.

(2) *Why abandon the collective defence policy?* Secondly, for what reasons are Governments such as the British, whilst remaining members of the League, not attempting, apparently, to restore confidence in the

League's guarantees of co-operative defence? What are the typical arguments by which those who dislike, or despair of, this policy seek to justify their attitude? (As I am speaking of Governments which are by no means pacifist, I shall leave out of account, in this context, the absolute pacifist's argument).

(a) "*Sanctions mean War.*" I expect you find, as I do, that the slogan most commonly used by those who want to annul the sanctions obligations, or to make it "optional," is that "sanctions mean war." This phrase is so used as to imply that if nations do not accept any obligation to defend anything except their own direct "interests" (which in Britain's case happen to extend all round the globe), they will thereby keep clear of war.

I must refrain from plunging into this far-reaching controversy. I will only say that I regard this argument as fallacious and the slogan as misleading. I must add, however, that there seems to me to be a strong case for the claim that the sanctions obligations are now too ill-defined, too unlimited, for a League which is so far from being universal. The critic asks: "How can you expect Britannia to make herself policeman throughout the world when adequate support is manifestly lacking? How can any Government accept for its peoples risks so ill-defined as those of Article XVI, in contingencies so unforeseeable?" An attempt was made, you remember, in Annex F of the Locarno Treaties, to define the sanctions obligations in such a way as to answer such critics without smashing the League's preventive and coercive power: but much has happened since Locarno and it may well be that the believers in collective security neglected for too long the task of re-defining the obligation. The broad principle to be sustained is clear enough. As Lord Cecil has put it, "All League members are properly charged with the duty of co-operating in whatever measures are found possible and effective to prevent and stop aggression."

(b) "*Collective Security has been tried and failed.*" Another contention which I expect we have all met is that the policy was tried, fairly tried out, in the Ethiopian case, and that it proved a failure. The League, it is said, proved incapable of fulfilling the task put upon it (as if it were an engine capable of functioning powerfully without so much attention on the part of the Member Governments as the refilling of the petrol tank). I shall assume that I need not spend time in demolishing that most injurious misrepresentation, especially after Senator Rolin's reminder of Sir Samuel Hoare's shameful secret bargain with M. Laval on September 10th, 1938—the day before Hoare's famous speech of September 11th calling for a full sanctions policy.* As the Emperor of Ethiopia pointed out in burning words to the special Assembly in 1936, what was lacking was not the strength but the will. If the British and French Governments in power at that crucial time had not been lacking in loyalty to the League's cause and if, I venture to say, they had not been blinded in their choice of risks by the old ways of thinking about the use of national power, the Italian gamble could have been prevented, almost certainly: failing that, it could have been discredited and stopped on terms that would have represented a victory for the collective peace system.

The claim that the sanctions system has been fairly

* See *Britain and the Dictators,* by R. W. Seton Watson, page 361 (Chapter X).

tried and proved a failure is a travesty of the truth, which we should be at pains to expose.

But the fact remains that the Governments chiefly concerned did not think fit either to use the threat of sanctions to prevent the Italian crime or to apply and maintain the sanctions to the extent necessary to protect the victim. Why did the British Government and the French make that disastrous choice?

(c) *"Britain was too weak."* The answer commonly given in public by those who think the right course was chosen is that the Powers supporting the League had not the necessary preponderance of strength and that, in particular, Britain had "cut her armaments to the bone," "disarmed to the edge of risk," and had neglected the most elementary precautions for the air defence of Malta.

Well, I recognise of course that a layman, an outsider, lacking the secret information available to a Government, is not in a position to assess such claims with full knowledge. But I must say that, having regard to the known strengths of the Powers in 1935, and having regard to the extraordinary dangers to which the Italian expedition was exposed at the far end of the Suez Canal, I find the claims absolutely unconvincing. (If they were justified, they would, incidentally, imply that the huge sums which Britain spent on armaments since the Great War had been used with gross incompetence; on this showing, many Ministers and officials ought to have been sacked and Sir Samuel Hoare ought never to have been allowed to score the personal triumph of his speech of September 11th, 1935.)

Frankly, I think the main, underlying reason why the British Cabinet shirked those risks was a different one.

They never really believed, most of them, in the principle of sanctions. (Remember Sir John Simon's revealing declaration that the Government would not have "risked a single British warship in a successful action *for the cause of Abyssinia.*") And they were gambling, with the Laval Government in France, on the chance of buying Mussolini's loyal partnership against German aggressiveness, at the price of condoning Italian aggression in Ethiopia. They did not want to embarrass or bring down the Fascist régime.

I have referred to these past events, not to cry over spilt milk, but because they show, I think, that we need a different Government in London if we are to have a resolute collective defence policy in future.

(d) "*The League is now too weak.*" That milk has been spilt: that injury to the League's cause has been done. And so now we meet the argument, more formidable than ever before, that the League really is impotent to deal with such a challenge as it now has to face. It is impossible now—so the argument runs—for the League to mobilise the preponderant power which would be needed to discourage future aggression by those who have pulled off such notable triumphs of violence. This truly is a decisive question. If the League cannot mobilise such preponderant power at present and if there is no chance of such preponderance being achieved in future, granted courageous democratic leadership, then indeed we are driven back, inescapably, to the purely self-regarding use of national power, and to the consequent crystallisation of exclusive private alliances between one group of tribes against another group. Back to tribalism.

Is it possible to make the League's sum come out?

In answering this fateful question, we have to beware of the blind optimist and the doctrinaire on the one hand, and of the defeatist on the other hand.

The optimist, in his desire to combat a desolating scepticism, may remind us that the League can still show a membership of over fifty states, representing four-fifths of the entire human race, and commanding between them a huge proportion of the world's economic and financial resources. But we must set against this the fact that, if a major European war flares up, the League Powers will have to meet a very formidable challenge, probably involving the concerted action of two or three great armed States. We must recognise, also, that scepticism about collective security has gone very deep : the liquidation of the League's open confederacy against aggression has spread very wide.

It is almost certainly true that, in general, the defender in modern land warfare, if equipped with material comparable to the attacker's, has a great advantage : but the development of the air weapon, especially since the end of 1933, has, at least apparently, given to the ruthless attacker an unprecedented power to strike a sudden, devastating blow at long range.

We must recognise, too, that the problem is no longer simply one of preventing war : there is also the much more difficult problem of stopping two wars and of ending the most desperate game of menaces that the world has ever seen. To-day, when nearly a quarter of the human race is at war, Mr. Clarence Streit has fearfully strong ground for his argument that the League has definitely failed in its primary task, the prevention of war, though it may still serve in the further task of stopping the war with the minimum of injury to civilisation. And to-day, when Austria has been subjugated and annexed, when German and Italian control of Spanish territories is being consolidated without any substantial restraint on the part of Great Britain, and when Germany is mobilised and incited to passion in order to terrorise Czechoslovakia, Captain Liddell Hart has much ground for his contention that, in a strategic sense, "the next world war" began two years ago with the invasion of Spain, and that we are losing, in Spain and elsewhere, positions that would be of decisive strategic importance when the struggle is extended.

Certainly, then, we have no justification for a complacent belief that it will be a quick and easy job to make the League potent. There is no short cut—"back to the Covenant," back to "a straight League of Nations policy." If a Government, genuinely convinced of the need for a working collective peace system, were to come into power in England next week, it could not rally the disarrayed League overnight, or avoid a difficult and dangerous transitional period; it would have to play an opportunist game in many respects, and would probably have to put up with some serious "casualties in lawful procedure." It would find, too, that any policy calculated to stop the armaments race would now involve a tremendous problem of economic readjustment and would clash with vested interests that have grown more powerful than ever before.

This is a formidable catalogue of obstacles which must be reckoned with. And frankly, I believe that unless the British and French Governments change their policy radically and quickly, the frayed remnants of League loyalty will snap, the old anarchic doctrines of "neutrality" will sweep away the beginnings of solidarity against aggression, and Europe will be submerged by the greatest of man-made disasters.

But I believe also that the stampede could be checked. The League's credit and authority could be so restored and extended that there would be a good chance even now of preventing Armageddon if . . . *if* the British and French Governments were to give a resolute democratic lead in favour of a return to League principles, if they were to treat Russia as a full partner in this effort, and if they were able to win something more than platonic sympathy from the United States. If the British Government pledges Britain to fight for France, *qua* France, irrespective of the cause for which France chooses to fight, then exclusive alliances will destroy the crippled League, and any moderate element in Hitler's Germany will be silenced by the argument that this is "encirclement" again. But if a British Government shows unmistakably that it will take risks, together with France and others, in resisting aggression, whenever such resistance can be made effective, then we may still expect to see a revival of faith that will bring to the League an assured preponderance of power.

(3) *Ensuring Collective Defence.* What policy, then, offers the best hope of making a reliable pooled defence against aggression?

I assume that, in the first place, we must obtain governments in London and Paris which sincerely, ardently, desire to achieve this.

Secondly, I assume that planned co-operation with Russia should replace the present frigid discourtesies.

Probably you share, as I do, the anxiety and repugnance widely aroused by the execution of so fearful a number of the leaders of the Russian enterprise. You may feel that the trials show that the régime must either be rotted through with treason or else helpless in the grip of a jealous and bloody tyranny. But Russia, nevertheless, remains, presumably, a Power of tremendous strength to-day, and still greater strength to-morrow: and she is, for solid reasons of "enlightened self-interest," indubitably and sincerely on the same side as Britain, France and America in the present stage of the struggle against the war-system. British relations with Russia should involve not frigid discourtesies but planned co-operation.

Moreover, we shall make another very grave mistake if we underestimate the importance of the collaboration and goodwill of the smaller Powers in Europe. Their interest in getting rid of the war-system is certainly not less than that of any of the stronger Powers: and, if we were simply making a calculation of strength, we should be blind to overlook their great economic power and the very considerable military strength of some of them.

In short, I share the view expressed by some who have preceded me, that some kind of Peace Bloc should be formed on the basis of the Covenant, open to all States which do sincerely accept certain obligations to co-operate in defence against aggression and contribute to advantageous services of peace.

We may find that one of the urgent tasks we shall have to undertake in the immediate future is to oppose the virtual abolition of the obligation to co-operate in any kind of sanctions against an aggressor. If the coming

Assembly declares that co-operation in sanctions is to be interpreted henceforth as purely "optional," the League will suffer a deadly blow, for which the smaller Powers, as well as the strongest Members of the League (and indirectly the United States), will bear a share of responsibility.

iii. *Re-organising Peace.*

Lastly, I will suggest a few examples of the kind of peace-building that we should set our hand to.

Many of the violent challenges of recent years have been suffered to succeed because there was, in truth, a certain moral weakness in the position of those who might have withstood these challenges. German rearmament and German militarisation of the de-militarised zone are cases in point. If violent challenge is to be avoided, those who should withstand that challenge must not be paralysed by a moral weakness in their own position. We need a certain "moral rearmament."

iii. (A) *The Peace Treaties.*

It would be desirable that the League Covenant should be separated from the Treaties of Peace: that the lie of Germany's sole war guilt should be repudiated, in so far as this has ever been responsibly alleged: and that the charge that Germany had shown herself unfit for any share in the responsibilities of Colonial administration should be withdrawn. Such moves may still have a certain psychological importance. For somehow, sooner or later, Europe must recover the co-operation of the moderate, more pacific Germany which built its hopes, at the end of the War, upon the honourable application of the principles laid down in President Wilson's 14 points. We must get back to those principles. We must negotiate with that Germany, on that basis, without the dictation which made the Versailles Treaty a rotten bond.

iii. (B) *Raw Materials.*

Next, what can be done to ease the problem of affording assured access to Raw Materials?

I need not stress the point that the Raw Materials problem is not primarily a Colonial problem but rather one which concerns the policy of the sovereign States. At present, States which are in a position to export Raw Materials are imposing almost no restrictions, discriminatively or otherwise, upon such exports. But this does not mean that there is no danger of restrictions or discriminations being applied in future: nor does it mean that there is no occasion to do anything about the matter. Indeed, the problem can most easily be handled before it has become more prickly. Would it not be desirable that the recommendations of the Raw Materials Committee of the League should be followed up by making an international convention which would guarantee access to Raw Materials on equal terms, subject to reciprocity. There should, however, be one reservation to any such engagement. The withholding of Raw Materials for a particular country should be recognised as legitimate when used as an international sanction for preventing and stopping breaches of the world's code of peaceful behaviour.

I recognise that this proposal is not as simple as it looks, but I think it is practicable and worth while.

Do not suppose, however, that an agreement of this kind would wholly remove the difficulties which Germany and Italy have been exploiting as a grievance. These countries have a real problem under present conditions. The problem arises primarily, of course, from the unalterable fact that Nature has not provided stocks of many of the main raw materials within these countries. We cannot alter what Marshall Graziani has called: "this perpetual and iniquitous sanction of Nature." But the situation is aggravated by such a currency policy as Germany has chosen to adopt. Germany's difficulty in obtaining raw materials from abroad is due almost wholly to her difficulty in obtaining adequate foreign currency with which to pay for them: and this in turn is affected by her armament policy. Would it not be possible to make provision internationally for some kind of barter system which would, for the time being, ease Germany's problem of obtaining foreign exchange?

You will at once think of an objection. Why should other countries exert themselves to facilitate Germany's imports if they know that the bulk of those imports will be used for the completion of an armament programme which they regard as menacing to themselves? No country will willingly strengthen the hands of another country which it regards as a prospective aggressor against itself. At every turn, in considering such proposals for the promotion of trade, we find ourselves involved in political questions that arise from the War system. Either the nations must work together as a Commonwealth or else they will seek to thwart each other as competing tribes. The promotion of economic welfare cannot be separated from the prevention of aggression: the positive and the negative sides of collective security are interlocked.

iii. (C) *Colonies.*

As regards the Colonial problem, I assume that you agree that a far-reaching and accelerated change is needed. We must not only move away from exploitation into real trusteeship but we must move much faster than hitherto away from trusteeship into real self-government for the Colonial peoples.

I suggest that Britain should make plain her willingness to accept the principles of an improved mandate system for all her non-self-governing Colonies not yet under mandate, at least in Africa to begin with. We must abandon the idea of making the Colonial Empire into a closed economic preserve. We must apply the principle of equality of trading opportunity, and we must do so, not as a concession to our friends or as an inducement to join the League, but because the principle is justified by its own merits and by the needs of the native peoples concerned.

We should go further. We should make an experiment in international administration of Colonial territory on a sufficiently large scale. Why should not Britain declare her intention to renounce sovereignty in favour of an international administration by the end of a certain period, such as twenty years, in the territory which comprises Kenya, Uganda, Tanganyika and Northern Rhodesia? During that period the greater part of the British personnel of the administration would be gradually replaced by personnel recruited from countries other than Britain. A similar experiment might perhaps be made in Oceania and the Southern Pacific, where the present system of government by a medley of sovereign states from afar has grown up haphazard and may be open to serious objection if judged impartially by modern standards of good administration. Some study has been given to this problem in the United States. (It must be remembered however that a previous experiment of this kind in the New Hebrides proved very unhappy.)

A great part of the Colonial problem is in reality a strategic problem, which can only be solved through the development of a collective peace system. And here I appeal to you, and especially to American friends, to consider President Wilson's doctrine of freedom of the seas. He laid down the principle, you remember, that the seas should only be closed, if closed at all, by international action for the enforcement of international covenants. In other words, Britain should never again be free to use Gibraltar as a blockade control for the coercion of her private enemies but should only do so as agent for the international community in restraining a Covenant-breaker. Unless and until that principle of shared responsibility for control of the narrow seas wins practical American support, I do not think that we shall be able to solve a great part of the Colonial problem. It may be argued that Britain is at present the most disinterested and fair-minded of the Powers which might hold such strategic points as Gibraltar, Malta and Cyprus. But that claim is not likely to commend itself to Mussolini, or indeed to a Greek who remembers the use Britain made of her naval power during the last World War. If we can regard the sea-ways as the world's highways rather than as private roads to be guarded, for private ends, by this nation or that, then a great part of the Colonial problem, now unmanageable, will become easy to solve.

iii. (D) *India.*

In conclusion I want to say a word about an enormous question which I am, I know, inadequately equipped to deal with.

I believe that the present situation in India cannot and should not be maintained. Within a short time, say five years, India should be free to control her own foreign policy and therewith her own defence. Great Britain should declare that she will renounce sovereignty in British India by the end of that period. A Constituent Assembly, for drafting India's new constitution, should be elected so soon as agreement can be reached upon a fair system of representation: and Great Britain should negotiate a Treaty with this Assembly.

I recognise, of course, that any such proposal presents enormous difficulties. We have not only British India to deal with. We have not only the point of view of the Indian Congress to consider. And the problem of representation is not yet solved. But I believe that no policy which is less radical than this can now meet the need. Indian nationalism has to be handled now with an extraordinary courage and imagination if explosive consequences are to be avoided. India's capacity to govern herself is being educated and proved in the Provinces. If we do choose the risks of setting India free to shape her own foreign policy we shall, I believe, find in that free India a powerful contributor to a collective peace system.

iv. *Conclusion.*

There remains the question, what should we do as individuals, if we believe that the policies of our respective countries should be directed towards creating conditions in which a collective peace system can work properly.

I will hazard only two suggestions.

To English members of the Institute I would say—" Get another Government—one which really believes in the principles of the collective peace system." (I recognise that this is not the kind of view which commonly finds expression here. But I have tried faithfully to avoid partisanship : this is a critical time : and I feel about this matter so strongly that I should not have been happy to contribute to this series if I had not been free to express this opinion frankly.)

I wonder if I can, without offence or impertinence, offer one suggestion to the Americans here. I believe that, if they want to see the power and influence of the United States used effectively as a contribution to a cause which is greater than America's, they should concentrate for the present upon securing such an amendment of the Neutrality Law as will enable the President to make the embargo policy discriminatory in the time of war.

For my part, I believe that, unless Britain, France and America quickly resolve to return a more civilised answer to the question : " For what shall our national power be used? " we shall soon see the greatest disaster that man has ever let loose upon himself.

CHAPTER XIII

THE LEAGUE AND THE WORLD TO-DAY

by

K. ZILLIACUS*

Former Member of the Information Section of the League of Nations Secretariat

MY subject is "The League and the World *To-day.*" But the present is only an invisible line dividing the past from the future. Therefore in order to understand the present we must analyse the past. That is mostly what I am going to do. I am going to try to review the history of the League in order to help us to understand why the League to-day is broken and discredited and the world is drifting to war. And I am going to suggest what we ought to do about it because I think something can be done and ought to be done.

What I have to say represents my own views only: the Secretariat cannot be held in any way responsible for those views. In fact, precisely because of the views I hold I have resigned from the Secretariat, to take effect in the near future. I do not think that the views I hold are compatible with remaining an official of the League—at least not as the duties of a Secretariat official are interpreted to-day.

That does not mean that I have in any way weakened in my belief that the things the League stands for are

* When I gave this lecture I insisted upon the private character of the meeting, as I was still—and had been since January 1920—a member of the Information Section of the League Secretariat.—K.Z.

things that are essential to the survival of civilisation. I believe that more than ever. But I think that the real fight to-day is on the home front and not in Geneva.

What I am giving you now is the distilled essence of reflections and observations stretching back for 19 years in the service of the League. I am afraid it will be a very bald summary. I shall have to put things dogmatically and briefly because there is no space to introduce qualifications and reservations.

i. *International Anarchy.*

I will begin with the question: Why was there a world war? I think the answer is: there was a world war because of international anarchy aggravated by imperialism. If you want to go deeper into what is meant by international anarchy I should recommend G. Lowes Dickinson's book *International Anarchy*. If you want to know what imperialism means I would recommend you to J. A. Hobson's *Imperialism*. Another useful book is Professor Parker Moon's *Imperialism and World Politics*, also Leonard Woolf's *Empire and Commerce in Africa*. If you still want more after that, try R. G. Hawtrey's *Economic Aspects of Sovereignty*. Briefly, international anarchy means that each state is a law unto itself, that its sovereignty is absolute in the sense that it does not recognise any international, political, legal or even moral obligation transcending its frontiers. Under international anarchy the highest duty of a government is to be a trustee for the national interests as interpreted by itself. In the service of those self-interpreted national interests it is not only entitled but obliged to take any action it thinks fit. In practice that means any action it thinks it can get away with, including war.

The natural result of international anarchy was that each state wished to be a bit stronger than any possible rival in order to be able to uphold its rights and interests against any challenge. That is sufficient to explain the arms race and the system of rival alliances. If you found you had common interests for the time being with some other states and that those interests were being challenged by a rival state or group of states, you made an alliance with the people who for the moment were in your camp. That was the game of power politics as played in Europe before the War. That game obliterated the distinction between self-defence and the use of war as an instrument of national policy. For it meant that states would go to war for their "honour and vital interests," each government being sole judge of what was meant by honour and vital interests and refusing to submit them to any form of arbitration. On honour in that form Lowes Dickinson in the book I quoted writes as follows: "Honour will only be defended by arms if, and when, it is believed to coincide with interest. It is, in fact, a word without content, employed to excite or to sustain emotions. Interest, on the other hand, has a content, though it may be questionable whether it has one worth fighting for."

ii. *Imperialism.*

Imperialism may be defined as the result of the development of capitalism in the conditions of international anarchy. About the last third of the last century there was a curious development in our economic system. There was a great concentration of economic and financial power at the top in the form of big trusts, combines, giant banks. The representatives of these great business and banking interests fused both socially and economically—socially through inter-marriage and the institution known as guinea pig directors, and economically through the diffusion of shares in business enterprises—with the old aristrocracy to form a new class: the plutocracy. The plutocracy supplied most of the funds for the chief political parties and owned or controlled the advertising in most of the press. The apparatus of state—the Foreign Office, the Colonial Office, the higher civil service, the commissioned ranks in the fighting services and their equivalent in the Church—were manned almost without exception from the ranks of those who belonged to the class that lives by rent, interest and profit. This class in turn became more and more dependent, both economically and socially, upon the plutocracy. The latter accordingly gained ever greater influence over the apparatus of state and the moulding of public opinion. Their self-interest became increasingly identified with the 'national interests' it was the duty of Governments to defend.

The books on Imperialism I have quoted show in detail how all this worked out in practice. The way it worked out was that these interests would exert pressure on governments and dope public opinion in their search for markets. Because it is a characteristic of our economic system that more and more markets are required if it is to function satisfactorily. This economic system is very good at expanding production, but is not nearly so good at getting the goods absorbed that have been produced. Hence the need for new markets.

In this connection I would recommend to your attention some of the remarks of Sir Arthur Salter in a series of lectures he gave last year in the United States and has published under the title of WORLD TRADE AND ITS FUTURE. He observes that the golden age of the capitalist system in the last century was a period of expansion. Private enterprise was continually opening new markets in North and South America, Africa and Asia, and developing them by a continuous flow of capital. He says that at home new markets were being created in the chief industrial countries by the rapid increase of their populations. To-day he says this process has pretty well stopped. There are no " new " territories which can be developed from outside. For now, each undeveloped territory is establishing its own industries or already pre-empted by an industrial power. The increase in population in Europe and North America, which was very considerable in most countries in the last century has slowed down to the point of stagnation. Sir Arthur concludes that what he calls middle-aged constipation is a characteristic failing of capitalism in its present state and the chief aperients—new markets abroad and a rising population at home—are no longer available.

The scramble for new markets that occurred in the last third of last century, and particularly the feverish competitive grabbing of territories in Africa, the process by which trade accompanied the missionary and the flag followed trade, inevitably involved conflicts of interests between the Great Powers whose nationals were engaged in this scramble. In other words, imperialism gave what you might call its aggressive contents to international anarchy.

It was the clashing interests of the plutocracy in the colonial scramble that constituted the bulk of the so-called conflicts of national interests about which the diplomatic crises revolved that culminated in the World War. There were, of course, other sources of friction, matters of prestige, national irredentisms, the desire for power for its own sake, etc. But the main drive behind the foreign policies of the Great Powers was their "defence" of the interests of their respective plutocracies. Moreover, the interests of the plutocracy soon included a direct vested interest in the arms race, because that was one way of making big profits. In all these developments the role of these plutocratic interests was not so much sinister as politically irresponsible. The social and international consequences of what they were doing did not interest them. All that they were concerned about was to earn as big and quick profits as possible, in whatever way came handiest. The net result of their activities was to multiply and exacerbate the clashes of so-called national interests, to drive up the arms race far beyond the point required even by power politics and to poison and bedevil public opinion by propaganda in order to secure support for arms expansion. This whole system ended and was bound to end in a world war. Capitalism did not create international anarchy, but it did help to make it unmanageable and to make the resulting war more devastating.

If you like to sum up in a metaphor the condition of the nations under international anarchy and imperialism, it is as though each nation represented a motorbus. The buses were driven by people who had no use for any rules of the road. They believed that the only way to drive through traffic was to threaten that, if anybody challenged their right of way, there would be a collision. Therefore, of course, each driver wanted as big and heavy a bus as possible, in order to frighten off others and to come out top if there was a collision. That was bad enough. But on top of that there was at the side of each driver a monomaniac on the speedometer—of profits. The maniac did not care a bit about the driver's troubles with the steering wheel and rival buses. All he cared about was the speedometer of profits. He had an obsession, amounting to a mania, a fixed idea, about stepping on the gas at all times and in all circumstances.

iii. *The World War.*

Under these conditions you would not be surprised if collisions were frequent and disastrous. They were frequent. There was a series of small wars and diplomatic crises and each one engendered a worse situation until finally the whole thing collapsed and crashed in the Great War.

In that war all the Great Powers concerned believed that they were defending themselves, but were in fact fighting a preventive war. Austria-Hungary was fighting to prevent the disruption of the Austro-Hungarian Empire by Serb nationalist propaganda and also to maintain her predominant position in the Balkan Peninsula. Russia was fighting to prevent Austria-Hungary from defeating Serbia, in which case the Berlin-Vienna axis would have had the upper hand in the Balkans and there would have been an end to Russia's imperialist aims for expansion through Constantinople. France went to war on the principle that if Germany and Austria-Hungary beat Russia they would be strong enough to turn on France next and strip her of colonies. Great Britain declared war on Germany because it was argued that, if the German-Austrian combination beat the Franco-Russian combination, Germany would be mistress of the continent and strong enough to make the British Empire stand and deliver when it came to colonies.

That does not mean that we were not entitled to take part in this game of imperialism and power politics in order to defend what had been acquired in the past. But it does mean that there was a tremendous gulf between what the common people thought they were fighting for and what the war was really about. Before the War there was no democracy whatsoever in foreign affairs. They were conducted just as secretly and autocratically in France and Great Britain as they were in Germany, Austria and Russia. And they were conducted solely in the service of the interests of the plutocracy and by a Foreign Office recruited from the upper classes.

Once the war had begun this gulf between what the rulers were fighting for and what the peoples believed it was all about deepened rather than lessened. One of the first things all the belligerent Governments did was to commit themselves to secret and entirely imperialist peace terms under the pressure again of the same plutocratic interests, reinforced by purely militarist War Office and Admiralty interests and by the need to bribe each other to go on with the war. In the case of the Allies these imperialist war aims were embodied in the famous

Secret Treaties providing for the division of the Ottoman Empire, recognising Japan's claim to the annexation of Shantung at the expense of China, France's desire to detach the Rhineland from Germany, Russia's hankering for a free hand in Poland, and Italy's greed for annexations and imperialist expansion both on the Continent and in Africa and Asia Minor. In the meantime, in public the Governments were saying that they did not want an inch of anybody's territory and that they were fighting for justice and democracy and a war to end war, to show that treaties were not scraps of paper, to protect small nations, to enthrone the rule of law, etc. As you realise, we pretty thoroughly lost the war on that basis.

iv. *How Morale was Maintained.*

As the war dragged on it became plain that it was not going to be like previous wars. It was not going to be short and sharp; it was a test of endurance. There was a military deadlock at the front and each state was reduced to inflicting the maximum of suffering on its opponents in order to break the morale of the common people. That was why Hindenburg said the war would be won by the people with the strongest nerves and Lenin said that the war would not be settled at the front, but in the rear. The central point of the fight on the home front in the different countries was the attempt by the governments to maintain the morale of their peoples, to make them believe they were fighting for a just cause, to kid them along.

The peoples had almost from the beginning adopted one big constructive idea as the way out. It began, I think, on the extreme left in England in the first few weeks of the War. That was the idea of a League of Nations, of some kind of world order to replace international anarchy and power politics. The idea spread rapidly. It was taken up almost immediately by the Liberal Government of that time. It became part of the public war aims and propaganda of the Allies. It was above all taken up by President Wilson. He was the main political force that put the thing through although—I think it is just to say that—when it came actually to working out the details of the Covenant his job was mostly that of editor and compiler, of putting together what came from other sources.

In both Governments and public opinion it was the left—progressive and radical opinion—that was most enthusiastic and convinced about the new idea, and the organised labour movement that gave it the bulk of its political support. The further one went to the Right, the more the professions of support for a League of Nations became half-hearted and half-headed.

v. *The Exploitation of Wilson.*

I want to dwell on certain features of what happened in the War. I have just been reading the records of those times and it is a tragi-comic business to read of the relations between the Allies and Wilson. Wilson kept on trying, from the moment the U.S.A. entered the war, to persuade the Allied Governments to come in with him on a statement of war aims that would commend themselves to liberal and labour opinion and to revolutionary Russia. The Allies steadily refused to commit themselves officially in any way. But Wilson kept on making public speeches in which he put forward his statements of war aims for the encouragement of public opinion. The Allies kept on exploiting these speeches, particularly in Great Britain, and with particular reference to the 14 points. The whole story is given in the *Intimate Papers of Colonel House.* You find, for instance, that on November 30th, 1917, House attended, at Wilson's orders, an inter-Allied Conference in Paris and for the third time made an effort to get the Allies to agree to a moderate statement of peace terms. The Allies would not do so. Thereupon, as House says, he consoled himself with the belief that "a comprehensive address" by the President might prove "the moral turning point of the war." It would re-assure liberal and labour opinion and perhaps keep the Russians in line. That was the origin of the 14 points speech. The Russians took rather a "tough" view. They said the Secret Treaties had not been repudiated and the speech was therefore humbug. But the 14 points were very successful with liberal and labour opinion.

vi. *The Hoodwinking of Labour.*

There is a further item. Mr. Lloyd George was at that time in some difficulty with the Trade Unions. It was a question of inducing them to release another 250,000 men for the front—and men who had been exempted. There is a telegram from Balfour, then Foreign Secretary, to House explaining that the negotiations had reached a deadlock. There was a danger of serious trouble and the whole point was to persuade the Trade Unions to release the 250,000 exempted men by making them believe that we were fighting for peace terms that they could agree with. Wilson was urged in the telegram to do his stuff again, that is to make a speech on the lines of his previous ones. Wilson had already decided to make his 14 points speech—partly as a counter-blast to the publication by the Bolsheviks of the Secret Treaties. Lloyd George had made a statement just before on similar lines to the Trade Unions. When he got the 14 points speech he came back to the Trades Unions and said that it was perfectly clear that we were fighting for nothing but the peace terms put forward by the Trades Union leaders, President Wilson and the British Government. On that understanding, those 250,000 men were released to be slaughtered. And yet the Governments did not give up their secret treaties and they had no intention of making a Peace Treaty based on the 14 points. What they tried to do at the Peace Conference was to get a peace as near to the secret treaties as possible, but couched in the language of the 14 points.

vii. *Intervention in Russia.*

The Dealings of the Allies with President Wilson and with labour were humane and honest compared to their dealings with the Russian revolution. There they first tried to support counter-revolution in the shape of General Kornilov. When that failed and when they had thereby helped to bring down the Kerenski Government, they got the Bolsheviks instead. When the Bolsheviks came in, the Allies decided on a policy—the Cabinet memorandum is quoted in Mr. Lloyd George's Memoirs—of on the one hand giving the Bolsheviks a number of assurances such as that the Allies had no intention of intervening in Russian internal affairs or of supporting counter-revolution, that they agreed to the principle of self-determination and of no annexations, etc. On the other hand, the same memorandum goes on to say that the Allies should proceed to supply arms, money and agents and advisers to the various white Russian Governments—the Cossacks, Persians, Caucasians, etc., and that they should do this very secretly so as to avoid the imputation, so far as possible, that they were preparing to make war on the Soviet Government. It was a perfectly deliberate cold-blooded policy of double-dealing.

According to the Cabinet minutes, Balfour, as Foreign Secretary, and Sir George Buchanan both declared that from the point of view of standing up to Germany in the East and of preventing German penetration in Russia the Bolsheviks were the best chance: they were the only people with backbone. They went on to say that, on the other hand, there were strong reasons for breaking off relations with them because of their revolutionary propaganda in all countries, including Germany. Sir George Buchanan went further and said that he would sooner see a rupture than risk Bolshevik propaganda in England, because it was so dangerous, being attractive to people who had nothing to lose.

As you know, there were efforts made at the time by the Government to try to prove that the policy of Russian intervention had nothing to do with class war motives. If one studies the official records and Cabinet minutes available to-day it seems to me that it is clear beyond any doubt that this policy of intervention in Russia was a class war policy undertaken even at the clearly realised risk of prolonging the world war and of strengthening our enemies in the world war.

The war itself came to an end how? It came to

an end, not through the Governments, but because the tortured peoples rose in revolution. They rose first in Russia. That example, stimulated by military reverses and starvation, fired the Germans and the Austro-Hungarians. The ground was quaking under the feet of the Allied Governments too. It was revolutions and not governments that ended the world war.

viii. *Wilson's Qualified Failure.*

At the Peace Conference there was the same struggle between these different factors that I have mentioned, *i.e.* the Allied Governments, Wilson and the section of opinion he represented, and the extreme left and the Russian Revolution. That struggle resulted in a compromise. There was a fairly harsh peace treaty : nevertheless not nearly so bad as the secret treaties would have made it. The secret treaties were largely put out of operation by the Russian revolution because they had relied upon the participation of Russia in order to carry them out. The whole moral climate created by the Russian revolution and by Wilson made it very difficult also to go beyond a certain point in turpitude.

If intervention in Russia had succeeded and we had had a Fascist Russia at the Peace Conference, I think the situation would have been very much worse. But it did not succeed. It failed not because the Allied Governments tardily realised that intervention was morally wrong and politically foolish but because of the resistance of the Red armies in Russia on the one hand and because of the threat of a general strike in Great Britain on the other if it was not stopped. Those are the facts.

The other half of the Peace Conference compromise

was the League of Nations. It emerged as a mere shadow of what Wilson, Smuts, Cecil and liberal and labour opinion had hoped it would become. I shall have more to say of that in a moment.

But first I want you to consider the question, why was it that the Peace Conference compromise was as bad as it was? Why in other words, did Wilsonism fail as lamentably as it has failed? For after all, looking back to-day in the light of all that has happened since, there is no doubt about it that it did fail. Why did the whole vast body of liberal and labour opinion, with the mighty American President at its head, accomplish so little, and that of such brief duration?

I can read you two quotations which I think give you a very clear picture of why "Wilsonism" failed. The first is from the diary of a member of the American delegation on the way across the Atlantic to the Peace Conference on the S.S. *George Washington* in December, 1918. He records a statement by President Wilson to the U.S. delegation:

> "The President remarked that we would be the only disinterested people at the Peace Conference, and that *the men we were about to deal with did not represent their own peoples*. . . . With great earnestness he re-emphasised the point that unless the Conference was prepared to follow the opinions of mankind and to express the will of the people rather than that of their leaders at the Conference, we should soon be involved in another *break-up* of the world, and when such a *break-up* came it would not be a war but a cataclysm."

That was what Wilson said before he arrived at the Peace Conference. This is what Colonel House wrote in his diary on March 3rd, 1919, at the Peace Conference:

> " It is now evident that the peace will not be such a peace as I had hoped, or one which this terrible upheaval should have brought about . , . If the President should exert his influence among the liberals and labouring classes, he might possibly overthrow the Governments in Great Britain, France and Italy; but if he did, he would still have to reckon with our own people, and he might bring the whole world into chaos. The overthrow of Governments might not end there, and it would be a grave responsibility for any man to take at this time."

That is, I think, a very interesting pair of quotations. The first one shows that Wilson sincerely believed—and he went on believing it to his dying day—that he was a democrat who preferred trusting the peoples to giving in to governments that did not represent their peoples. It also shows that he realised clearly that, unless a decent peace were concluded on the lines that the peoples wanted and not on the lines of the unrepresentative Governments, there would be another war, and it would not be a war but a cataclysm.

The second quotation shows what happened when the President was up against it, when he realised that the Governments were betraying him and the peoples. He was obliged to choose finally between acquiescing in what the governments were doing or breaking with the governments in order to tell the peoples the truth. He preferred betraying the peoples that had trusted him and throwing in his lot with the governments that had double-crossed both him and the peoples.

Why did he do it? Not because he thought the peoples might not listen to him, but on the contrary, because he was afraid that they would take him at his word if he told them the truth and would overthrow the Governments that had done this awful thing.

I believe that is the root cause of the fatal weakness of Wilson and of the whole vast body of " middle-of-the-road " progressive opinion he represented. When it came down to brass tacks they preferred knuckling under to what Conservatism and plutocracy were doing rather than to part company with them finally and to fight the plutocracy and come down on the side of the common people and the revolutionary movement on the left.

That does not mean that it would have been an easy business to go left in this way. In those days the revolutionary movement was narrow-minded, fierce, dogmatic, arrogant, full of hatred of progressive opinion and of ambitious illusions. It would not have been an easy job. But my point is that the job was not even attempted and the results were what they were.

Just as Wilson during the War had consoled himself each time he failed to get the Allies to agree to his peace terms by making a statement of his own on the subject and hoping that in due course his wishes would be father to the Allies' thoughts, so at the Peace Conference he and all the opinion that he represented, that lib-lab, middle-of-the-road, well-meaning, and woolly-minded, opinion, consoled itself for having to knuckle under to the reaction rather than to break with it by believing in a brilliant victory in the future for the moral forces whose defeat in the present they were deploring. They read into the very loose and weak Covenant of the League, which was all the reactionaries would agree to accept, far greater virtues and powers to change the future than the facts warranted, because it was only by such hopes that they could buoy themselves up in the disappointment and the defeat that they had suffered. With Wilson and the opinion he represented it was very much a case of hope deferred maketh the heart grow fonder.

ix. *The League and Liberalism.*

For the first ten years of the League it looked as though the philosophy, the idea on which the League was based, this liberal conception of the future, were going to be justified. I must explain a little bit what that idea was.

The League was an attempt at world government and that attempt was to be based on social justice and on democracy.

The reference to social justice occurs in the introduction to the constitution of the International Labour Organisation, which says that universal peace is impossible unless it is based on social justice and that conditions of labour exist in the world such as to breed discontent on a scale dangerous to world peace. But that reference was made rather perfunctorily and simply as an attempt to placate the feeling in the working class. No one took it very seriously.*

On the other hand, the emphasis on democracy was very great. It was in fact the key to understanding the liberal conception at the Peace Conference of the future of the League. It was believed that the war marked a further stage in the triumphal march of democracy which had been advancing from West to East ever since the American and French revolutions. The belief at the

* For proof of this assertion, see Temperley's *History of the Peace Conference of Paris,* Vol. II, pp. 32-3.

time seemed reasonable. Because, as General Smuts wrote in his pamphlet at the Peace Conference :

> " The old institutions on which imperialism and autocracy flourished lie crumbled in the dust; a great wave of advanced democracy is sweeping blindly over Europe."

The prevailing system of government in the world, and therefore in the League, was going to be political democracy on the economic and social foundations of capitalism. I would also read to you what Smuts said in his broadcast from the League Wireless Station in January last :

> " The Covenant . . . simply carries into world affairs that outlook of a liberal, democratic society which is one of the great achievements of our human advance. Perhaps that is the real reason why the new dictators object to it."

x. *The League and the Ideological Conflict.*

The conclusion I wish you to carry away from this summary up to date is that the League was from the outset in a triple sense the result of taking sides in an ideological conflict. In the first place it was a result of the victory of the Allies in what they regarded as an ideological conflict between democracy and imperialism. There was a great deal of propaganda in that antithesis but it became more nearly true by the end of the War owing to the revolution in Russia and the entry of the U.S.A. But that conflict was conducted horizontally, between classes, in each belligerent country as well as vertically between the two belligerent camps.

In the second place, the League was the outcome of a conflict of the right and left at the Peace Conference.

Roughly the Covenant represented the maximum concession made by Conservatism and plutocracy at the Conference to Wilson and the liberal wing of the British delegation and to the public opinion they represented, who used as their chief argument the danger of working class revolution unless guarantees were given against a recurrence of war (the League) and for more social justice (the I.L.O. and promises at home).

In the third place, to use Wilson's famous phrase, the League was intended to "make the world safe for democracy." In short, in its working out and in its purpose the League was intended as a form of world government to guarantee and make the world safe for the kind of civilisation that is based on social justice and democracy.

But when it came to working out that idea, the Covenant did not go very far. It is a very loose document. It is meant to be half-way between a super-state and international anarchy but I think it is nearer to international anarchy. There is not only the minimum of obligations in the Covenant but they are self-interpreted and decisions of substance, as apart from procedure, have to be unanimous.

The legal obligations were few and self-interpreted. But the assumption was that a higher moral code was going to prevail in future. As Wilson put it at the Peace Conference:

> "Nations must in future be governed by the same high code of honour that we demand of individuals."

Or as House said:

> "The agreement or promise of a power shall be inviolate."

The change from power politics to that conception

would have been nothing less than a moral revolution. Why was it believed that such a change was possible?

The reason was that the World War had been such a horrible thing that for a long time to come there would be a passionately convinced public opinion that wanted to make a success of this new code of international conduct and of this new system. It was believed that there would be an effective majority of opinion in an effective majority of states in an effective majority of disputes which would regard the upholding of the Covenant and the strengthening of the League's authority as a matter of honour and vital interests. In other words, defending the Covenant against aggression would, it was thought, be treated by the Governments, under the pressure of public opinion, as a major national interest. "Honour and vital interests" were going to acquire a popular context. Democracy was going to invade foreign affairs and to insist upon collective security against war as the greatest of all the interests of the common people.

That was the view of the future taken at the Peace Conference by liberals. It was a noble and intelligent view, for it relied on the operation of reason and good-will. I think if one has any kind of belief in a democratic civilisation one has got to take that kind of view of human nature. It is an optimistic view but it is very far from a foolish view. On the contrary, it is a politically wise and a morally courageous view.

But the whole conception had one flaw which I am afraid has proved fatal. I think in the light of subsequent events we can put our finger on the flaw. I will read what Canon F. R. Barry says about that in *What Has Christianity to Say?*:

> "The collapse of the pre-war liberal creed was due to no mistake in its 'ideals.' Its ideals were right, and they are still valid. Its mistake was rather that it underestimated the irrational, instinctive, subterranean forces which thwart and destroy 'rational' human progress. Liberals forgot the historical determinism of economic and material pressure; they forgot the moulding power of social inheritance."

The liberals in other words overestimated the reality or the possibility of democracy under our existing economic system. They thought there was much more democracy than actually existed or could exist in a society divided into economic classes with conflicting interests. They forgot the reality of the class cleavage between what Disraeli called the two nations of the rich and the poor. They forgot that in foreign affairs it was only the interests of the rich that had counted and that those vested interests would bitterly fight any attempt to subordinate them to the general interests of the people. They forgot that the interests of the plutocracy are not the same as those of the common people. They took it for granted that the social and economic system was going to continue to function after the War very much as it had done before: that is with private enterprise as the main-spring although no doubt with more and more social reform.

xi. *The Great Slump and the Drift to War.*

That assumption held good roughly until the great slump. The League grew and became stronger during those years. But the slump was the sign that there was something radically wrong with our social and economic foundations. Sir Arthur Salter describes in *World Trade and the Future* how the great slump precipitated "the sudden and devastating collapse in the economic life of the world, in its financial system, in parliamentary government, in the new structure of peaceful international relations." "The vast reconstruction effort of the post-war world," he adds, "was directed to the re-establishment of the pre-war system with the one notable addition of the League of Nations. . . . Failure came because that system was in several respects inappropriate to the new conditions and because it was too weak to resist and control the new and greater forces that had developed within our economic and political system."

What happened in the slump? First of all, a further increase in the strength of finance and monopoly, capitalism, the power of plutocracy. Second, the use of their power by the plutocracy to keep going in the conditions of the slump by plunging their governments into economic nationalism, into war preparations, and into political reaction. As a consequence of these developments there was a greatly sharpened class conflict. That conflict has grown steadily in intensity until to-day it dominates the whole international as well as the domestic scene and is the crucial factor in world politics as in home affairs.

The capitalist counter-revolution began in Italy after the post-war slump, and then in Germany and Japan in the great slump. In those countries you have had a smashing of the whole constitutional framework and the emergence of dictatorial regimes as a sort of preventive counter-revolution by the plutocracy, allied for the purpose with gangsterism and invoking the religion of nationalism. Those regimes are of their very structure necessarily aggressive regimes because they cannot solve their social problems and appease the social discontent that brought them into being. In Germany and Italy, for instance, since 1932 the standard of living has sunk by about 20 per cent. and in Japan by about 30 per cent. If you cannot provide bread you have got to provide blood and circuses. The Fascist regimes cheated instead of satisfying the revolution complex and so had to turn it into a war complex.

In the Soviet Union—you have got to judge it against the background of what existed before and not by comparison with the West—there has been a real social revolution carried out at a fearful cost, which was greatly increased by the intervention policy of the Allies and the subsequent boycott of Russia. Therefore the revolution complex in that country has been changed into a reconstruction complex. The standard of living really is rising, the people are getting better off, culturally and politically as well as materially, as compared with what they had before. The U.S.S.R. wants peace because any war or threat of war is a disturbance and a drain on the resources of the country. They want to husband those resources in order to get on with the work of reconstruction.

In the democracies you find a condition of division and hesitation precisely because the same struggle between left and right, representing the workers and the plutocracy respectively, is going on in those countries and is now dominating both home and foreign policy. The Right is torn between its uneasy awareness that Fascist Imperialism will sooner or later demand colonies from *e.g.* France or Great Britain, and its desire to use the war-preparation and aggressions of Fascist powers as the only way of maintaining the atmosphere of fear and the feverish arming on which it has come to rely for survival. These things are not realised consciously so much as felt instinctively. But the sense of class-solidarity with the Fascist regimes and class-dislike of the Spanish workers, of the anti-Imperialist Chinese and the anti-colonial Abyssinians, not to mention the U.S.S.R., has undoubtedly warped and weakened British foreign policy.

xii. *The Need to Take Sides.*

The conclusion to draw I think is that to-day the old liberal idea that you could build up a League of Nations, a form of world government, however loose, by co-operation between all states and between all classes and parties within the state is unfortunately not feasible. We have got to abandon that idea. But the original conception, the idea that civilisation cannot survive unless it is based on world government, democracy and social justice, I think is still the only right idea and is the only path that we can possibly follow unless we are tired of civilisation.

I think the events of the last few years have brought out more clearly than ever the close connection between democracy, social justice and establishing some form of world law and order or world government. But I believe that to begin again with that conception, which is the only possible alternative to drifting into a world war, we have got to take sides in the ideological conflict. We have got to realise that that conflict has its roots in the claim of the working classes for social justice and in the resistance to that claim of the plutocracy.

If we try to sit on the fence in that struggle, we are in fact taking the side of the defenders of the social *status quo*. We have to choose and we do choose, whether we know it or not. Willy-nilly, we are actors in, not spectators of, the world drama.

I think the foreign policy that follows from that kind of view of the world is the foreign policy of going ahead with such States as are still within the League and as are prepared to come into a peace bloc or group based on far-reaching economic and political co-operation, on a square deal to colonial populations, on direct international representation of parliaments as well as governments, and on mutual assistance against aggression. In case of disputes, the members of this group would accept arbitration in their relations with each other and with all other states.

The group would offer the Powers that remained outside, and particularly the Fascist powers, any kind of guarantees they wanted within reason that they would not be attacked, that there would be no interference in their internal affairs, that we would co-operate with them economically and financially if they also gave guarantees against aggression and we would welcome them all the way in to our group if they would come in and as far as a quarter or a third of the way in if they would not come any further.

xiii. *How to Make a New Start.*

We would be primarily concerned with raising the standard of living within this group of nations and with common protection against aggression. But the group would have no kind of ambition to impose its ways on others—except that they would always be welcome to join. All the group would try to do in world affairs would be to stop the interference with other nations that is going on to-day from the Fascist Powers and particularly the armed interference in Spain and China and the France, Great Britain, the U.S.S.R., Czechoslovakia,[*] be part of a policy for reviving the authority of the League under the collective leadership of this group. For France, Great Britain, the U.S.S.R., Czechoslovakia, Spain, and, with reservations on military sanctions, the Oslo group, would form a powerful nucleus round which the League could gradually be re-consolidated. The belt of new States in Central Europe would rally to the leadership of the group so soon as they saw that it had re-captured the initiative in world affairs and could really confer security against aggression. The economic co-operation and diplomatic support of the United States would not be long in forthcoming.

The drift to war would first be slowed up, then stopped, and finally reversed. Step by step we should recover the ground lost in the disastrous years since Japan was suffered to smash the Covenant and occupy Manchuria. The Fascist States would first have to abandon aggression and then would gradually find they were losing their internal cohesion.

[*] The fact that Mr. Chamberlain has handed over Czechoslovakia to Hitler wrapped up in the cellophane of the Covenant and a scrap of paper (the Franco-Czech alliance) thoughtfully provided by M. Bonnet, makes the proposed policy more difficult and success more remote in time. It also emphasises the time necessity of removing the National Government. But world government based on social justice and democracy still remains the only possible objective of a civilised foreign policy, and the main lines of that policy must still follow the course indicated.

That is not an easy policy nor a policy free from risks. It calls for every bit of statesmanship and courage of which we are capable. But after all *noblesse oblige.* England has a record in history and a position in the world to-day that means we must either lead the nations out of the present mess or incur an unenviable share of the responsibility for a world war that will shatter the British Empire and destroy what we mean by civilisation.

It is none of our doing that we are faced by the choice between those tremendous alternatives. But it is our duty to look facts in the face and to recognise that those are the only alternatives to-day and that we must choose, and choose quickly. If we will the end we must will the means, and recognise that all who mean business with peace must come down in home affairs on the side of the workers and their struggle for social justice and real democracy and against the plutocracy and their defenders, just as in international affairs it is necessary to be for the ideology of world government and against the ideology of power politics.

To refuse to take sides would be to repeat in an even more disastrous form the tragic error of Wilson, and to open the flood-gates to Fascist barbarism. Democracy must make peace by solving the problems of world government and social justice, or perish in Armageddon. Instead of the cowardly, question-begging formula of not taking sides in the ideological conflict, the democracies have got to make up their minds to *win* the ideological conflict. For on the outcome of that conflict depends the future of civilisation.

APPENDIX

CONTENTS OF PROBLEMS OF PEACE
(Twelfth Series)

Appendix

CHAPTER IV

The Breakdown of the System of Collective Security. By Dr. G. P. Gooch.

- i. Survival of the Sovereign State
- ii. Imperfections of the Peace Settlement
- iii. Incompleteness of the League
- iv. French Policy, 1918-1924
- v. Failure to agree on Armaments
- vi. The Economic Slump
- vii. Failures to stop Aggression
- viii. Unwillingness for Peaceful Change.

CHAPTER V

World Co-operation on Health. By Dr. M. D. Mackenzie, Health Section of the League of Nations Secretariat and formerly Acting Director of the Singapore Epidemiological Bureau.

- i. Introduction: the Necessity for International Collaboration in Medicine
- ii. The Establishment and Methods of Work of the Health Organisation
- iii. The Malaria Commission
- iv. The Sleeping Sickness Commission
- v. The Leprosy Commission
- vi. The Cancer Commission
- vii. The Collection of Information from various Countries with regard particularly to Disease Incidence
- viii. Collaboration with various Governments
- ix. Medical Educational Work, including Collective Study Tours, Individual Study Tours and International Courses in Public Health Subjects
- x. Conclusion.

CHAPTER VI

World Economic Survey. By Dr. J. B. Condliffe, Member of the Economic Intelligence Service of the League of Nations Secretariat.

- i. Unheeded Warnings

CONTENTS OF PROBLEMS OF PEACE
(Eleventh Series)

i. Why We are Drifting to War
ii. The Economic Depression and the World Peace Crisis
iii. The Need for a New Start
iv. What Great Britain should do.

CHAPTER III

A French View of the League of Nations. By Gaston Riou, Secretary of the Commission of Foreign Affairs of the French Chamber of Deputies.

i. Introduction
ii. The Present State of Europe
iii. The Beginnings of the League of Nations
iv. Reasons for the League's Defeat
v. Conclusion.

CHAPTER IV

Central Europe and the Future of the Collective System. By Stephan Osusky, Minister of Czechoslovakia in Paris.

i. Introduction
ii. Three Different Conceptions of the Functions of the League of Nations
iii. The Situation To-day—Is Neutrality Possible?
iv. The Armaments Race
v. The Principle of Responsibility
vi. The Problem—With Special Reference to Central Europe
vii. The Independence of the Central European Powers: A Condition of European Security.

CHAPTER V

The Third Reich and the Future of the Collective System. By Dr. Fritz Berber, Director of the Research Department, Hochschule fur Politik, Berlin.

i. Introduction
ii. The Relationship of Germany to the League of Nations
iii. The Necessity for Peaceful Change
iv. Sanctions and Regional Pacts
v. Conclusions.

Appendix

CHAPTER VI

The Soviet Union in International Affairs. By Andrew Rothstein, Geneva Correspondent for Tass News Agency.

i. Imperialist Aims Renounced
ii. Illustrations
iii. Peaceful Co-existence with Capitalism
iv. The Fight for Peace
v. Always with Peaceful States
vi. Against Treaty-breaking
vii. Regional Pacts
viii. Ready for Defence.

CHAPTER VII

The United States of America and Sanctions. By Phillips Bradley, Associate Professor of Political Science, Amherst College, Massachusetts.

i. The Background of Recent American Foreign Policy
ii. The Legal-Political Position of the United States
iii. The Economic Consequences of American Neutrality
iv. Public Opinion and Collective Security
v. The United States and the Future of Collective Security.

CHAPTER VIII

The International Labour Organisation and the Future of the Collective System. By E. J. Phelan.

i. Peace a Pre-condition of International Collaboration
ii. A Dangerous Definition
iii. The People and the League
iv. Attempts to Gloss the Covenant
v. National Reactions Resulting from International Failure
vi. A Basis for the Future
vii. Alternative Possibilities.

CHAPTER IX

Economic Nationalism as a Necessary Contribution to a World Collective System. By R. J. P. Mortished, of the International Labour Office.

CONTENTS OF PROBLEMS OF PEACE
(Tenth Series)

v. The Struggle for the Outlawry of War
vi. Collective Organisation
vii. Organising Peace
viii. Peaceful Settlement of Disputes
ix. Peaceful Change
x. Disarmament
xi. Collective Security
xii. Conclusion.

CHAPTER IV

International Law after the Covenant. By Dr. H. Lauterpacht, Reader in Public International Law in the University of London.

i. The Development of International Law
ii. The Covenant
iii. The Function of International Law.

CHAPTER V

Modern Europe; Joint-Editor, *British Documents on the* Associate Professor of International Law in Princeton University.

i. The Particular Relevance of the Problem To-day
ii. Prevailing Trends in American Foreign Policy
iii. The First Trend—Intensification of Isolation
iv. The Second Trend—Genuine Interest in the Cause of Peace
v. How far is America Prepared to go in Effective Collaboration with the League?
vi. The Chief Trend—Anxiety to keep out of War
vii. Proposed Changes in the Policy of Neutrality
viii. A Summary of the American Attitude—the Compromise Neutrality Bill
ix. The Future of American Neutrality
x. Conclusion.

CHAPTER VI

Peace in the Far East and the Collective System. By Dr. Guy H. Scholefield, O.B.E., Librarian, General Assembly Library,

Appendix

CHAPTER X

The Future of the Collective System. By C. A. W. Manning, Professor of International Relations in the University of London.

i. "The Collective System"—A Term of Art?
ii. Collectivism. A Novelty?
iii. The Watchword of this Investigation
iv. An Article of Faith
v. The Existing Framework of Collectivism
vi. The Given Social Milieu
vii. The Traditional Basis of Association
viii. The Traditional Legal Order
ix. A Problem *Sui Generis*
x. The Super-State. A *Sine Qua Non?*
xi. Must the Covenant be Amended?
xii. Collectivism and Force
xiii. Will War become Unthinkable?
xiv. The Settling of Disputes—An Unsolved Problem
xv. Wanted: A New Ethic?
xvi. A New Ideology?
xvii. The Conclusion of the Whole Matter
xviii. W(h)ither Sovereignty?

CHAPTER XI

The Future of the Collective System. By P. J. Noel-Baker, author of *Disarmament;* formerly British Delegate to the Assembly of the League of Nations.

i. Introduction
ii. The Main Principles of a Practicable System of Collective Security—Universality of Purpose and Scope
iii. The Universality of the Vital Interests of Nations
iv. The Limitations upon the Universality of Scope
v. Further Principles of the Collective System
vi. What Law is required as a Foundation for an Effective System of Collective Security?

CHAPTER XII

Economic Co-operation as the Basis of Economic World Order.

CONTENTS OF PROBLEMS OF PEACE
(Ninth Series)

Appendix

CHAPTER II

Small States in the League of Nations. By William E. Rappard, Professor at the University of Geneva, Director of the Graduate Institute of International Studies, Geneva.

i. Great Powers and Small States before the World War
ii. Small States and the Covenant
iii. Small States within the League
iv. Small State Policies?

CHAPTER III

The Great Powers in the League of Nations. By Alfred Zimmern, Montague Burton Professor of International Relations in the University of Oxford.

i. Relations between the Great Powers as the Essential League Problem
ii. The Great Powers in the Covenant
iii. Force and Law as Elements in the League System
iv. Democracy and the League.

CHAPTER IV

French Foreign Policy. By Etienne Dennery, Professor at the Institut des Hautes Etudes Internationales, Paris.

i. General Tendencies and Particular Anxieties
ii. Franco-German Relations
iii. Disarmament
iv. Security
v. Eastern and Central Europe.

CHAPTER V

The Socialist View of Peace. By the Rt. Hon. C. R. Attlee, M.P.

i. Capitalism, Nationalism and War
ii. Weaknesses of the League System
iii. Armaments and the Collective Peace System
iv. Loyalty to the World Commonwealth: the Proposed Peace Pact.

CHAPTER VI

"Pacifism is Not Enough." By Sir Norman Angell, author of *The Great Illusion*, etc.

CHAPTER VII

CHAPTER VIII

CHAPTER IX

Appendix

CHAPTER X

National Economic Planning and International Organisation. By Robert MacIver, Professor of Political Science, Columbia University.

i. The Logical Problem of Organisation
ii. The Principle that Technological Advance necessitates International Order
iii. Misconceptions of Economic Planning
iv. In Economic Planning the State Assumes but does not usurp a Function
v. The Practical Breakdown of the Principle of Economic Automatism
vi. The Proper Function of Centralised Controls
vii. The Nature, Necessity, and Limits of such Controls in our Present Civilisation
viii. Economic Planning and National Self-Containedness
ix. National Economic Stability More Attainable within an International Order
x. The Nemesis of National Self-Containedness
xi. Economic Planning and International Trade.

CHAPTER XI

Financial Aspects of the "New Deal" in the United States in some of their International Implications. By Dr. Leland Rex Robinson, President of the International Securities Corporation of America, and Lecturer on Finance, Columbia University.

i. The First and Second Post-War Economic Crises
ii. Remedies for Economic Discontent
iii. Currency Doctoring and Credit Manipulations in the New Deal
iv. Alternating Attitudes towards Foreign Countries
v. Some Mutually Inconsistent Objectives
vi. Some Significant Results
vii. International Repercussions and the Outlook for the Future.

Appendix.

Volumes i—v were published by the Oxford University Press; Volumes vi—xii by George Allen and Unwin Ltd.